Common Birds
of Nunavut

Mark L. Mallory

Mallory, Mark L.

Common Birds of Nunavut / written by Mark L. Mallory

Published by Inhabit Media in collaboration with the Nunavut Department of Education and the Nunavut Wildlife Management Board

Text in English

ISBN 978-1-927095-66-9

Cover photo © W Lynch/Arcticphoto
Cover and book design by Atiigo Media Inc., Iqaluit, Nunavut

Printed in China

© Inhabit Media Inc. 2013

Library and Archives Canada Cataloguing in Publication

Mallory, Mark Laurence, 1965-, author

Common birds of Nunavut / written by Mark L. Mallory.

"This book is an updated version of Birds of Nunavut, published in 1997"--introduction, page 9.
Includes bibliographical references.
ISBN 978-1-927095-66-9 (pbk.)

1. Birds--Nunavut. I. Wyndham, M. Birds of Nunavut.
II. Title.

QL685.5.N86M34 2014   598.09719'5   C2013-908618-8

Common Birds
of Nunavut

Written by Mark L. Mallory

Credits

As with all of the books in this series, it would not have been possible to produce this book without the financial support of the Nunavut Wildlife Management Board, the Government of Nunavut Department of Culture, Language, Elders and Youth, and the Government of Nunavut Department of Education.

Photographs were graciously provided by Karel Allard, Lindsay Armer, Shawn Craik, Sebastien Descamps, Lynne Dickson, Cameron Eckert, Darryl Edwards, Mark Elderkin, Kyle Elliott, Charles Francis, Grant Gilchrist, David Hussell, Dana Kellett, Nadine Lamoureux, Jim Leafloor, Carolyn Mallory, Mike McEvoy, Dennis Minty, Anders Mosbech, Rolf Nagel, Norm North, Mark Peck, Lisa Pirie, Jennie Rausch, Jim Richards, Gerald Romanchuk, Tyler Ross, Dorothy Tootoo, Ray Wilson, and Credence Wood, in addition to those taken by the author.

Much of the local ecological knowledge presented in this book borrows from the local ecological knowledge compiled by Eva Arreak, currently the Premier of Nunavut, in the first *Birds of Nunavut*, by J. S. Wendt and M. Wyndham. The other local ecological knowledge included in this book was largely gathered by Jason Akearok through projects undertaken with Mark Mallory.

This book is dedicated to Manasie Audlakiak (1948-2013) and Winston Fillatre (1949-2013), members of the Nunavut Wildlife Management Board who truly personified the Vision of the NWMB: *"Nunavut: A world-class model for the cooperative management of healthy wildlife populations."* Manasie and Winston were particularly strong advocates of conservation education, and enthusiastically supported the development of this book. They would have been so pleased with the results.

Acknowledgements

In my opinion, the books that comprise this series are excellent educational tools and unique and informative souvenirs for tourists who visit this wonderful territory. I have been very pleased to be involved with this series to date, serving mostly as a technical and writing editor on two books. The people that have made this book, and in fact the entire series, possible have been: Neil Christopher, Gwen Frankton, Carolyn Mallory, Jim Noble, and Tony Romito. I hope that readers will recognize the tremendous effort and dedication that this has taken, through the shifting priorities and financial constraints of each individual's various organizations, as well as the demands on their personal lives. It is truly laudable.

For this book, I am indebted to my colleagues at the Canadian Wildlife Service for much of the knowledge on birds that I have acquired through working with them, in particular: Jason Akearok, Karel Allard, Birgit Braune, Kathy Dickson, Andy Didiuk, Garry Donaldson, Alain Fontaine, Tony Gaston, Grant Gilchrist, Siu-Ling Han, Vicky Johnston, Dana Kellett, Jim Leafloor, Craig Machtans, Kevin McCormick, Jimmy Noble Jr., Mia Pelletier, Jennie Rausch, Greg Robertson, Myra Robertson, Paul Smith, Ian Stirling, and Steve Wendt. Outside of the CWS, I have benefitted greatly from discussions with and insights from Josh and Kelly Boadway, Shanti Davis, Mark Forbes, Mark Maftei, Aevar Petersen, Ib Krag Petersen, Mark Wayland, and Pat Weatherhead. Jennie Rausch provided valuable unpublished data to allow me to update range maps of some species in Nunavut. In fact, the species range maps shown in this book provide the most current and verified ranges available for many of these species, thanks in large part to the work and contributions of people listed above. Numerous discussions with Inuit guides and assistants during fieldwork, as well as consultations with communities, greatly improved my understanding and appreciation for Inuit local ecological knowledge of birds. Laura Legge, Carolyn Mallory, and Katherine Wilson assisted greatly with edits. In getting to where I needed to go to study or view these birds, I am grateful for the logistic and financial support of Environment Canada (CWS), Indian and Northern Affairs Canada (NCP), the wonderful staff at Natural Resources Canada (PCSP), and Adventure Canada.

Finally, it would not have been possible to undertake all of this Arctic adventure without the bottomless support of my wonderful family: Carolyn, Conor, Jessamyn, and Olivia. They have been there for me through all of my long field trips, the weekends at work, the blizzards and water rationing, and our collective warm tropical breaks in the depths of winter. I could not ask for a better bunch to call my own. Thanks, guys!

About the Author

PHOTO: DENNIS MINTY

Mark Mallory moved to Iqaluit in 1999 with his wife, Carolyn (author of *Common Plants of Nunavut* and *Common Insects of Nunavut*), and three children, Conor, Jessamyn, and Olivia. He has had a lifelong passion for birds, and knew he was going to be a bird biologist in grade three. Fulfilling that dream, Mark received his M.Sc. studying the effects of acid rain on wildlife in Ontario, before the Arctic beckoned. In Nunavut, Mark worked as a seabird biologist with the Canadian Wildlife Service, giving particular attention to marine birds in the High Arctic, and using both western scientific information and local ecological knowledge from Inuit communities to research and monitor birds of that area. He received his Ph.D. conducting studies of the northern fulmar, one of the most fascinating birds in this territory. This is the first book that Mark has written solo, although he was recently an editor and contributor for *A Little Less Arctic*, a scientific book that discusses how climate change is affecting top predators (marine mammals and birds) in Hudson Bay and Foxe Basin. Mark has authored over 140 scientific papers and book chapters, and he and Carolyn are regular resource staff on Arctic cruises, discussing birds, plants, and northern living. Mark and his family moved from Nunavut to Nova Scotia in 2011, where he currently holds the position of Canada Research Chair in Coastal Wetland Ecosystems at Acadia University. Wherever the rest of his journeys take him, Mark will always feel at home in the endless horizon, grey mist, and incessant winds of an Arctic seabird colony . . . watching for polar bears sneaking up on him.

Dedication

For my nestmate, Carolyn, and my brood, Conor, Jessamyn, and Olivia

PHOTO: GRANT GILCHRIST

Table of Contents

Introduction

The pages that follow will introduce you to the fantastic world of birds in the territory of Nunavut, Canada. This book is an updated version of *Birds of Nunavut*, published in 1997. A new resource was needed as, recently, more people are looking at birds in Nunavut for a variety of reasons. Scientists are keenly interested in birds because the environment of Nunavut is changing in so many ways (community growth, industrialization, climate change, contaminants, tourism) that can adversely affect wildlife, and many birds serve as sentinels of the health of the environment. As well, since the 1990s, there has been an increasing desire to learn from the local knowledge of Inuit, which has again put a spotlight on birds. Tourism, especially from cruise ships, has increased dramatically in Nunavut since the 1980s. While most tourists come to see bears,

PHOTO: MARK MALLORY

FIGURE 1

whales, icebergs, and Inuit communities, guaranteed attractions are the massive seabird colonies on the cliffs of Lancaster Sound, Hudson Strait, and Baffin and Ellesmere Islands (Figure 1). Finally, most of the birds in Nunavut migrate out of Canada for the winter, which means that they are international citizens. Canada is a signatory to international agreements for the management of migratory birds, and this has taken on new importance when we consider recent global concerns such as disease transport (e.g., avian influenza), effects of environmental catastrophes (e.g., Deepwater Horizon oil spill in the Gulf of Mexico), or garbage and other pollution dumped into our oceans (e.g., chronic oil and bilge water dumping offshore from Newfoundland). For all of these

PHOTO: MARK MALLORY

FIGURE 2

reasons, a new version of the book was necessary as an educational tool for a wide audience.

Everyone is familiar with birds (Figure 2). We see them in villages, hamlets, and cities, on or over the highest mountains, along the coast, and in the most remote parts of the tundra. We go fishing and see them on or around lakes and rivers. We go hunting for seals or whales and see birds on the ocean. They are on television, posters, postage stamps, and aircraft. We see them eating seals, lemmings, and bugs, or ripping apart garbage bags. We see them from the most southern part of James Bay to the North Pole. Birds are so widespread and common that it is easy to take them for granted and forget how specialized they are and what remarkable feats they accomplish during migration.

This book is intended to serve as a guide to the most common birds in Nunavut, and to provide some interesting details on their lives specifically in this territory, including their historical and cultural ties to Inuit, their status and the threats they experience, and, in some cases, their future.

The species selected for this book were chosen based on the following criteria:

1 They were or are important to Inuit as food and/or cultural resources;

2 They are likely to be seen near communities, along coastlines, or by tourists; or

3 Their population numbers are declining, so spotting one or a flock may be unlikely, but if it did occur, that observation would be very important to report.

There are close to 10,000 species of birds in the world, in all habitats, from deserts to tundra. The number of bird species found in an area declines as one moves from the equator to the poles. The environment is less harsh and more stable near the equator, and consequently the diversity and stability of habitats is greatest in the tropics, allowing for the evolution of bird species that can exploit small niches (how an organism makes its living in its environment). In contrast, polar environments are highly seasonal, with much reduced development of vegetation (which provides habitat and food) and long periods of darkness and cold (which make it difficult to feed), leaving relatively few niches for birds to exploit. Thus, of the thousands of bird species in the world, only 268 have been observed in Nunavut, and of these, exactly half (134 species) are known to breed here, according to the revised *Birds of Nunavut: A Checklist* (Richards and White, 2008).

A Brief Primer on Birds

What makes a bird a bird? Probably the most common answer would be that *they have feathers.* All modern birds have feathers, and they are the only modern animals to have them. However, we know from fossils that some dinosaurs had feathers. It's through this fossil record and comparative anatomy that we believe birds evolved from reptiles.

In many ways, birds might be the easiest of the broad groups of vertebrates (animals with backbones) to distinguish. There is great diversity in the appearance or reproductive strategies within fish, amphibians, reptiles, and mammals. Birds, on the other hand, are fairly homogeneous (similar).

Here are a few keys to identifying birds:

✓ All birds have feathers and wings, even if they cannot fly.

✓ All birds have bills (sometimes called beaks), and lack teeth.

✅ All birds lay eggs.

✅ All birds are endothermic (warm-blooded).

Below are less obvious but also important characteristics that all birds possess:

✅ All birds have four-chambered hearts.

✅ All birds have lightweight and/or fused bones.

✅ All birds have furculae (wishbones) that prevent their chests from compressing during flight.

As well, most birds have exceptional navigational skills and many have complicated communication behaviours, which includes the production of songs.

Feathers, the most obvious, common feature of birds, serve three important functions. First, feathers enable the bird to fly by creating a broad but light surface for the wing to push against, or glide through, the air. Flight is not unique to birds—mammals (bats), insects, and even some fish can glide or fly, but birds are the only animals that fly using feathers. Second, feathers provide insulation for birds, especially the downy feathers located close to the body, underneath the outer contour feathers. These feathers trap air between the skin and outer feathers, reducing heat loss from the bird. In some cases, these feathers can also reduce heating of the skin or body by blocking the sun's rays. Finally, feather colouration provides birds with the ability to be very bright (usually to attract mates or to alert other birds to the limits of a territory), or to be camouflaged (to hide from predators). When you flip through the pages of this book, look at the photographs of the red phalarope (*Phalaropus fulicarius*) or the female common eider (*Somateria mollissima*), and you will get a feel for the diversity of bird colouration in Nunavut.

A trait that is *not* found in all birds is the ability to fly. All birds that live in or visit Nunavut can fly, but this is not the case worldwide. Many species are flightless. Perhaps the best-known examples of flightless birds are the ostrich (*Struthio camelus*) from Africa, the kiwi (*Apteryx* spp.) from New Zealand, and the penguins (family Spheniscidae) from the southern hemisphere. Flightless birds are usually found on islands that historically lacked mammalian predators or competitors. During past centuries, many sailors slaughtered these easy-to-catch birds for food—the dodo (*Raphus cucullatus*), for instance, or the great auk (*Pinguinus impennis*)—and once explorers and settlers introduced mammals (e.g., rats, cows, goats, and rabbits) to these islands, many of the flightless birds became endangered or went extinct.

Did You Know?

A common misconception we see in cartoons and on greeting cards is that there are penguins in the Arctic. Think of how many times you've seen a greeting card with a penguin *and* a polar bear on it! In fact, penguins are only found south of the equator, but through a process of convergent evolution (through which species evolve to have similar appearances to one another, but do not share common ancestors), murres look like penguins. A big difference is that murres can fly! (Figure 3)

PHOTO: MARK MALLORY

FIGURE 3

What Do Birds Eat?

We can tell a lot about a bird by what it eats. This tells us in part what type of habitat it will live in, what special adaptations it might possess, and what it might look like. Based on normal or typical feeding behaviour, we can classify a bird as falling into one of several feeding groups: herbivore (plant eater), carnivore (animal eater), omnivore (plant and animal eater), and scavenger (waste or scrap eater). As you'll learn by reading about some of the species, few birds always eat the same thing—they can switch diet through the year or even within a season. Nonetheless, these broad groups provide bases for classifying the typical types of food eaten by different bird species.

Herbivores

Animals that eat plants are called herbivores. These birds eat mostly plants, including seeds, berries, leaves, and sometimes roots. Among birds of Nunavut, the best examples of herbivores are geese, swans, and ptarmigan.

Carnivores

Animals that catch and eat other animals are carnivores or predators, and this is the feeding strategy of most birds of Nunavut. You are probably familiar with the most obvious predators—the falcons, hawks, and owls—which swoop in and capture birds, fish, or small mammals. But we tend to forget that other birds are principally predators, too, preying on smaller or less obvious animals. Often carnivores may feed on one type of prey for part of the year, then switch to another, or may simply feed on what is most abundant at the time. In fact, there are all kinds of carnivores, and they can be grouped according to the types of organisms they eat:

Piscivores

The seabirds (murres, fulmars, and guillemots) and loons are piscivores, meaning that they principally hunt fish, though they will also eat squid and marine worms.

Planktivores

Some birds are planktivores, meaning that they hunt zooplankton (tiny, shrimp-like organisms that can be extremely abundant in the ocean). The dovekie (*Alle alle*), a tiny seabird, eats zooplankton almost exclusively. Phalaropes (small, ocean-feeding shorebirds) also rely on zooplankton for much of their diet.

Kleptoparasites

Some birds (in Nunavut, the best examples are seabirds known as jaegers) steal food from other seabirds that are flying back to their nests. They might steal the food by ripping it directly from the bird carrying it, but often they chase and harass a bird carrying food until it drops it, and then they swoop in and take the dropped items. Stealing food like this is called kleptoparasitism. Jaegers eat fish, large plankton, bird eggs, and lemmings.

Molluscivores

The shorebirds (plovers and sandpipers) don't look very fierce, but they hunt zooplankton and mollusks along coastal areas, and also insects and spiders in upland areas. This means that they are molluscivores (mostly eating mollusks) and/or insectivores (mostly eating insects), depending on where they are feeding and the time of year.

Insectivores

Insectivores are birds that mainly eat insects. In Nunavut, these tend to be small songbirds like buntings, longspurs, and sparrows, but many of the waterfowl consume insects as well as other prey.

Benthivores

Benthivores eat animals that live on the bottom of lakes and oceans, such as sea urchins. Most sea ducks in Nunavut are benthivores.

Omnivores

Organisms that eat both plants and animals are referred to as omnivores. For example, humans are omnivores. Many of the small birds in Nunavut (buntings, redpolls, pipits) are principally insectivores, although they may eat some seeds and berries as well.

Scavengers

Finally, some birds in Nunavut are scavengers—animals that eat other dead animals or sometimes plants or garbage. The best-known scavengers in Nunavut are gulls and the common raven (*Corvus corax*). Common ravens survive in great numbers over the winter in Nunavut by scavenging food from local dumps.

What to Look for When Viewing a Bird

Birds come in a broad range of shapes and sizes, all adapted to the different ways that they exploit their environment to survive. However, there are a few key, simple parts of birds that you can observe to try and help you identify which species you are looking at.

BILL (or beak): One of the first features we see on a bird is its bill. The shape of the bill is adapted to the feeding style of the bird. When observing a bird, you should check to see how long the bill is compared to the rest of the head, and also pay attention to its colour. Other things to note about the bill are whether it is flattened (as in ducks); narrow or thick; short, stubby, long, or hooked (as in birds of prey); and whether there are any odd features like ridges, tubes, or serrations.

FEET AND LEGS: Like the bill, the feet and legs of a bird tell you a lot about its lifestyle. Does the bird have webbed feet (a bird that spends a lot of time in the water), thick and muscular toes with sharp claws (usually a bird of prey), or long and thin legs (usually a wading bird)? The colour of the skin on the feet can also be an important clue as to the identity of the bird.

TAIL: The shape of a bird's tail can be very distinctive in two ways. First, the tail can be forked, flat, or pointed. Second, the pattern of the feathers on the tail will often include unique stripes or different colours.

WINGS: The shape of bird wings varies tremendously. Try to see whether the wing is broad or narrow, long or short, and pointed or rounded. For example, rock ptarmigan (*Lagopus muta*) have relatively broad, short, and rounded wings designed for rapid, explosive takeoffs and manoeuvring. In contrast, northern fulmars (*Fulmarus glacialis*) have comparatively narrow, long, and pointed wings designed for efficient, long-distance flight and soaring.

EYES: Look carefully at the eye colour, and whether there is a coloured ring around the eye. This often gives information about the species, in particular the bird's age. For example, some gulls may have relatively dark eye colouring when they are young, but it brightens as they age and mature.

Types of Bird Bills

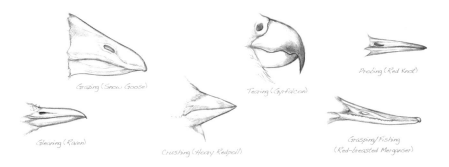

Grazing (Snow Goose)

Gleaning (Raven)

Crushing (Hoary Redpoll)

Tearing (Gyrfalcon)

Probing (Red Knot)

Grasping/Fishing
(Red-breasted Merganser)

Types of Bird Feathers

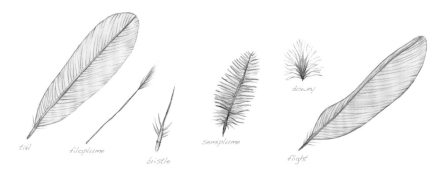

tail

filoplume

bristle

semiplume

downy

flight

Types of Bird Feet

Scratching

Grasping

Running

Webbed

Perching

How We Name Birds

If you've read the sections above, you'll notice that after the name of a bird species (what is referred to as the common name), there are two words, usually in brackets and italics. Those words form the scientific name of the species in Latin. Since no countries or people speak Latin anymore, it is considered a dead language, meaning that it does not change.

Birds, scientists, and bird watchers are found around the world, where there are hundreds of different languages. With all of these different languages and birds, how can people know they are talking about the same species of bird (or plant or animal)? Even among communities in Nunavut, the same organism can have different names, or the same name can refer to a variety of organisms. For example, in Inuktitut, some people say *nauja* to refer to the herring gull (*Larus argentatus*), or the Ross's gull (*Rhodostethia rosea*), though sometimes it just means gull.

In 1735, Carl Linnaeus of Sweden solved the problem of having many names for the same animal by developing a system to classify all living organisms, giving each a two-part Latin name. This is called binomial nomenclature. This system is used for all plants and animals, so that despite what language we speak, people (*Homo sapiens*) know we are talking about the same species. Usually in a book or scientific paper, the scientific name is included the first time a species is mentioned, but is not included after that.

Taxonomy and Families of Birds in Nunavut

Like all organisms, species of birds have been classified into larger groups based on similar or shared characteristics, a process known as taxonomy. For example, the full taxonomic classification of one of Nunavut's seabirds, the northern fulmar, is:

Kingdom	Animalia
Phylum	Chordata
Class	Aves
Order	Procellariiformes
Family	Procellariidae
Genus	*Fulmarus*
Species	*Fulmarus glacialis*

In this example, the very specific group (*Fulmarus glacialis*) refers to only one kind of bird, but there is more than one species that falls into the broader genus grouping *Fulmarus*, and there are many more types of birds in the family Procellariidae. The groups get larger until they include all animals (the kingdom Animalia).

Since the time of Linnaeus, we have much more scientific information available on different species, such as genetic information. This means that scientists can further split species into subgroups, sometimes called *subspecies* or *races*. For example, the common eider is *Somateria mollissima*, but in Nunavut there are different races of eiders: *S. m. sedentaria*, *S. m. borealis* and *S. m. v-nigra*. In these cases, we use the first letters of the species name and then the race to identify which bird we are talking about.

When scientists or bird watchers talk about birds, they often refer to groups at the order or family level. In Nunavut, you could see species from about 50 bird families (if you were lucky!), but when it comes to common birds that breed here, you might encounter species from 18 families:

Family **GAVIIDAE**: Loons—large, long aquatic birds adept at swimming and diving but awkward on land.

Family **PROCELLARIIDAE**: Fulmars—medium-sized seabirds with chunky, stubby bodies, superficially resembling gulls, but with tubes on top of their bills.

Family **ANATIDAE**: Ducks, geese, and swans—medium- to large-sized aquatic birds with long necks, flattened bills, and dense plumage.

Family **ACCIPITRIDAE**: Hawks—large, soaring birds with broad wings; powerful, hooked bills; and strong feet with large talons.

Family **FALCONIDAE**: Falcons—large, swift birds with long, pointed wings; strong, hooked bills; and powerful feet with large talons.

Family **GRUIDAE**: Cranes—very large, tall, slender birds with long legs, elongated necks, and long, straight bills.

Family **CHARADRIIDAE**: Plovers—small- to medium-sized, plump shorebirds with short necks and bills, and large eyes.

Family **SCOLOPACIDAE**: Sandpipers and phalaropes—small- to medium-sized, slender shorebirds with narrow bills and long legs, which are often observed in flocks.

Family **LARIDAE**: Jaegers, gulls, and terns—small to large, somewhat stout, web-footed aquatic birds.

Family **ALCIDAE**: Auks—medium-sized, short-necked, stout marine diving birds with rapid wingbeats and webbed feet.

Family **STRIGIDAE**: Owls—large birds with flattened faces, large eyes, and hooked bills on their broad heads, and sharp talons on their toes.

Family **ALAULIDAE**: Larks—small groundbirds that typically travel by running, and have long, pointed wings; short, slender bills; and a musical song.

Family **CORVIDAE**: Ravens—large, dark, stout birds with tapered bills.

Family **MUSCICAPIDAE**: Wheatears—small songbirds with slender bills, long tails, and long legs.

Family **MOTACILLIDAE**: Pipits—small, slender songbirds with thin bills, long tails, and lengthy wings. They are found in open country, and often wag their tails up and down while walking.

Family **EMBERIZIDAE**: Sparrows and buntings—a very diverse family of small- to medium-sized, stout songbirds with cone-shaped bills.

Family **FRINGILLIDAE**: Finches—smallest of the common songbirds in Nunavut; appear dainty and puffed up, with short, stubby, pointed bills.

Family **PHASIANIDAE**: Ptarmigan—plump, medium-sized, chicken-like birds with short, broad wings, short bills, and feathered feet.

Conservation and Protection of Nunavut Birds

Migratory birds in Nunavut are protected legally under the federal *Migratory Birds Convention Act*, the *Canada Wildlife Act*, and the *Species at Risk Act*, as well as special acts and regulations pertaining to the trading of wildlife and wildlife parts. Non-migratory birds, as well as raptors and corvids, are protected under the territorial legislation of the *Nunavut Wildlife Act*. People who wish to study or handle birds in Nunavut must first get appropriate permits, according to these pieces of legislation.

There are areas in Nunavut that have been protected specifically to conserve birds and their habitats. These are principally migratory bird sanctuaries (MBS) and national wildlife areas (NWA; Figure 4), and as of 2013 include: Seymour Island MBS, Prince Leopold Island MBS, Dewey Soper MBS, East Bay MBS, Harry Gibbons MBS, Queen Maud Gulf MBS, Bylot Island MBS, McConnell River MBS, Hannah Bay MBS, Boatswain Bay MBS, Akimiski Island MBS, Nirjutiqavvik NWA, Polar Bear Pass NWA, Niginganiq NWA, Qaqulluit NWA, and Akpait NWA. Bird habitats are also protected in national and territorial parks.

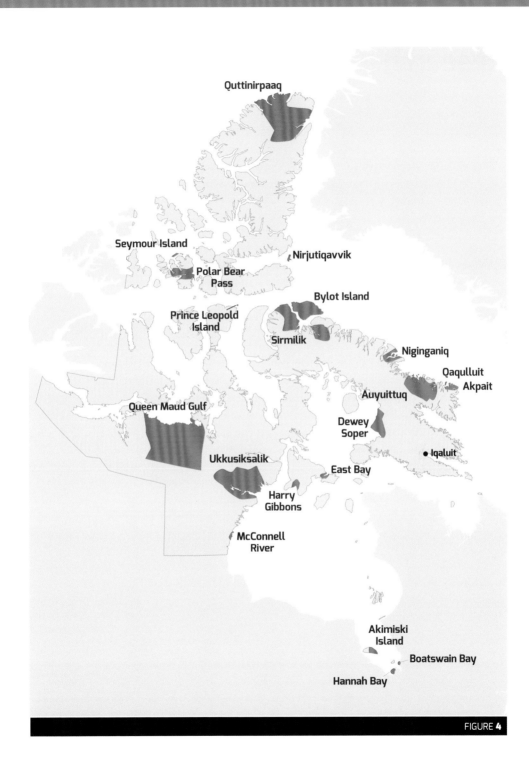

Quttinirpaaq

Seymour Island

Nirjutiqavvik

Polar Bear Pass

Bylot Island

Prince Leopold Island

Sirmilik

Niginganiq

Qaqulluit

Akpait

Auyuittuq

Queen Maud Gulf

Dewey Soper

• Iqaluit

Ukkusiksalik

East Bay

Harry Gibbons

McConnell River

Akimiski Island

Boatswain Bay

Hannah Bay

FIGURE 4

Research on Nunavut Birds

Inuit and their predecessors have lived in Nunavut for centuries, acquiring and passing on local ecological knowledge of birds and other wildlife so that hunters and their families could survive. This knowledge was particularly important for colonial birds (seabirds, sea ducks, and geese), which occurred in large numbers in predictable locations every year. By knowing these locations and the timing of the arrival and nesting of the birds, Inuit families could move to these areas at certain times of the year to find a guaranteed food supply. Thus, the first research on Nunavut birds should rightly be attributed to Inuit.

Additionally, many of the European explorers, from the 1600s onwards, recorded or captured birds on their voyages and brought them back to museums in the countries of their benefactors. These specimens can still be seen in museums today, hundreds of years after their collection. Much more recently, scientists have given more focused attention to certain birds in Nunavut. They want to learn about bird populations, migration routes, and interactions with other wildlife and humans to better understand the pressures and threats that bird species face. This will help scientists keep bird populations healthy.

Most of the bird monitoring and research in Nunavut has been initiated and conducted by national and international government organizations, including the Smithsonian Institution, the Canadian Museum of Nature, and particularly the Canadian Wildlife Service, although certain universities have also contributed substantial research on Arctic birds. The greatest research attention has been given to geese, particularly snow geese (*Chen caerulescens*), since they migrate to southern areas and are hunted throughout their range. However, seabirds, notably the thick-billed murre (*Uria lomvia*) and the common eider, have also been studied intensively since the 1970s. Since 2000, shorebirds have begun to receive more attention because populations of more than half of the shorebird species that breed in Nunavut are declining. Finally, in some locations, such as Rankin Inlet, peregrine falcons (*Falco peregrinus*) have been at the centre of research efforts.

What do scientists try to find out about birds? You could say *everything*. The more we know about the day-to-day life of birds in Nunavut, the better we can understand what affects bird numbers and breeding success. Some of the main questions scientists try to answer about Nunavut birds are: How many are there? Are their numbers going up or down? Where do they go in the winter? How long do they live? What do they eat? What eats them? What are the most important locations in Nunavut for these species' survival? What factors cause birds to fail at nesting?

To answer these questions, scientists, university students, and Inuit community members spend a lot of time watching birds. They hide in blinds far from the birds and watch through telescopes to gather the types of information they need (Figure 5). As well, there are other important techniques that scientists use to collect the essential information needed to answer the questions above. Perhaps the best-known technique is bird banding, where a small metal or coloured plastic band is attached

FIGURE 5

PHOTO: MARK MALLORY

FIGURE 6

around the leg of a bird (Figure 6). The date, time, and location where the band was attached are recorded and that information is inputted into an international database. If that bird is caught or seen anywhere in the world, the observation can be phoned or mailed to the people who manage the database, and scientists can tell where the bird moved to when it left Nunavut, and also how many years elapsed since the bird was banded. This technique works very well for birds that are hunted, like ducks and geese, because hunters are happy to send in the leg bands from their dead birds. In other cases, where birds are unlikely to be shot or handled, we need a simpler technique, where a person can just look at a bird and get the information on its band. For some birds, like geese, neck collars were developed (Figure 7) so that geese with coloured and numbered neck collars could be observed and the information on them recorded, without ever having to be touched. Similarly, unique combinations of coloured plastic bands on birds' legs can also be recorded and reported (Figure 8).

How do scientists observe birds that are almost never near humans—for example, birds that stay far out at sea, like fulmars? Since the 1990s, scientists have attached tiny recorders and transmitters to these species, to gather information on where the birds travel and, in

PHOTO: MARK MALLORY

FIGURE 7

PHOTO: MARK MALLORY

FIGURE 8

PHOTO: MARK MALLORY

FIGURE **9a**

PHOTO: KAREL ALLARD

FIGURE **9b**

PHOTO: KYLE ELLIOTT

FIGURE **9c**

some cases, what they do there. Included in this technology are geolocators, satellite transmitters, and depth recorders (Figures 9a, b, c, d). We can now follow birds as small as 30 grams—the size of a snow bunting (*Plectrophenax nivalis*). Information from this microtechnology has revolutionized our ability to track and understand the habitat needs of birds, and is a critical tool in the conservation of birds and their habitats.

PHOTO: NORM NORTH

FIGURE **9d**

Value and Uses of Nunavut Birds

Birds that breed in Nunavut have long been valuable to Nunavummiut and people elsewhere in the world. Utmost in importance is that, for centuries, birds migrating from Nunavut have been harvested and eaten as part of the diet of Inuit and First Nations people, as well as Greenlanders and North and South Americans. More than 13 million ducks and 3 million geese are estimated to have been killed by hunters in 2008 and 2009 in Canada and the United States, many of which had bred in Nunavut. Within Nunavut, Inuit harvested at least 39,000 birds and 30,000 eggs each year between 1996 and 2001.

In the past, the harvest of some species in North America was excessive and some species were harvested to extinction, like the Eskimo curlew (*Numenius borealis*), which once bred in western Nunavut. International agreements were signed between Canada and the United States of America early in the twentieth century to protect birds and their habitats. This helped many bird populations recover, and led to the formation of protected areas in places like Nunavut. But this is not just an issue of the past, and monitoring of harvested species needs to continue. Since 2000, research, monitoring, and consequent management decisions by Canada and Greenland have been focused on ensuring the sustainable harvest of shared common eider populations, which were declining due to overharvesting in Greenland.

South of Nunavut, people derive great value from birds by simply watching them—bird-watching is a multibillion dollar industry. In Nunavut, increasing numbers of tourists, particularly on cruise ships, are coming to view birds. (Figure 10). Outside of Nunavut, many people still hunt waterfowl (many of which come from Nunavut), hunting being one important use for birds.

PHOTO: MARK MALLORY

FIGURE **10**

In Nunavut, birds have had many traditional uses, other than simply providing food. Some of these include:

Warm clothing: Down, especially from eider nests, was and continues to be used in parkas as insulation.

Other clothing: In some areas, particularly the Belcher Islands, bird skins (especially eiders) were used to make *qulittaq*, or skin parkas, when there were not enough caribou skins. Some skins (notably those of loons) were also used to make *piniraak* or slippers worn inside *kamiks*, and skins of other birds like black guillemots (*Cepphus grylle*) were used as children's slippers.

Containers: Duck and gull feet were stitched together to make containers, or were sometimes inflated and used as children's toys. In some areas, bird skins were carefully sewn together and used to store various materials like tinder (to start fires) or sinew for sewing.

Brooms: Wings were stretched open and dried, and then used to sweep dirt from homes (*igluit* or *qarmait*), tents, and boats.

Towels: Skins, especially those from gulls, jaegers, guillemots, and ptarmigan, were used by hunters to wipe their hands after butchering animals or after eating.

Training: Young boys would learn to hunt by trying to kill small birds like snow buntings with stones (Figure 11).

PHOTO: MARK MALLORY

FIGURE **11**

It is important to remember that most birds in Nunavut migrate out of the territory and thus are only there for part of the year. Many Nunavut birds spend most of the year elsewhere (September to May), meaning that they are in another province or country for longer than they are in Nunavut. They have uses and value in their other homes, too! What people do in these other places has a direct effect on Nunavut birds—this could be hunting the birds, changing their habitats, or affecting the food they eat. For example, many of Nunavut's shorebirds migrate along coastal North America to winter in Central and South America. All along this route, development of coastal areas is reducing the traditional habitats needed by shorebirds to feed and rest. They survive in these areas and then return north the following year. As another example, most of the pollution that gets into the food chains of Nunavut birds comes from industrial and urban areas far to the south. This is why we need to study and understand what birds need to survive, and what places and habitats are most important for them, so that provinces, territories, and countries can work together to conserve and protect areas for birds. We must insist that those countries (and Nunavut) incorporate sustainability into their land development.

Threats to Nunavut Birds

Nunavut is a huge territory, and often seems even larger because the population is small, and it takes a long time to get from one community to another. Nunavummiut are lucky that so much of their land remains natural—this is different from most places in the world inhabited by people today. However, the lands of Nunavut are changing, and those changes may pose threats to the birds that live there. Birds and other wildlife are neither aware of these threats nor can they speak for themselves about the problems that people cause for them. Therefore, people must be aware of these threats and ensure that they reduce or remove them, to conserve and protect birds and other wildlife in this territory.

A few of the major threats to the birds of Nunavut are:

Climate change:

There are many ways that a warming climate is already affecting birds in Nunavut:

- **Mismatch of breeding times and food supplies.** With sea ice melting earlier in the year, food supplies necessary for rearing young marine birds like thick-billed murres (*Uria lomvia*) are more abundant sooner. Murres cannot adjust the timing of their breeding to keep up with this, and the result may be reduced breeding success.

- **Changing food supplies.** Warmer temperatures are changing foods in Arctic ecosystems, which may have a negative effect on birds. For example, ice-associated Arctic cod used to be the most common food for murres in northern Hudson Bay, but as the ice melts, cod have been replaced by capelin that live in the warmer water. A comparably sized capelin contains less energy than an Arctic cod, and thus adult murres have to work harder to provide the same amount of energy to growing chicks.

- **Parasites.** In some cases, existing parasites like mosquitoes are more abundant earlier in the year because of warmer temperatures. The combination of the mosquitoes' blood-sucking and the greater heat can kill nesting birds or cause them to abandon their eggs. Scientists are also worried that parasites that were formerly excluded from the Arctic, such as some ticks, may now be able to survive here with warmer temperatures. This could introduce new diseases to Arctic populations.

- **More frequent and intense storms.** While Arctic birds are adapted to withstand stormy weather, an increase in precipitation, especially wet snow or freezing rain, will cause increased nest failure for some species.

- **New competitor species.** Many communities are seeing birds that were not seen previously, like American robins (*Turdus migratorius*) or lesser black-backed gulls (*Larus fuscus*). These southern species might outcompete local species for food, causing the populations of local species to decline in the future.

Industrial and community development:

Inevitably, development, no matter the scale, leads to a change in or loss of bird habitats. Development can have the following consequences for birds:

- **Loss of habitat.** New infrastructure (mines, breakwaters, ports, roads, aircraft landing strips, buildings, etc.) requires physical changes to Arctic habitats, which can lead to substantial habitat loss in small parts or cumulatively.

- **Increased pollution.** Any human development leads to increased pollution of one form or another, including noise, garbage, and light pollution. Depending on the species, birds may be negatively affected by any or all of these.

- **Predator and competitor attraction.** Development activities generate garbage, which means food for scavenging animals like foxes and ravens. These types of animals often become more common near development sites. In turn, these scavengers can also eat birds that would normally live there, as well as their eggs.

- **Disturbance.** Development can increase disturbance due to noise from vehicles and the new activity undertaken by the development (mining, power generation). Some birds are sensitive to being disturbed while they are breeding and may abandon the area due to disturbance.

Increased shipping activity:

More ships, and ship activity for a longer period through the year, are expected if the ice-free season is longer in the future. The effects of increased shipping activity are the same as industrial development, except that they are restricted to the marine zone.

Contaminants and garbage pollution:

Nunavummiut, and Inuit in particular, are keenly interested in the contaminant levels of country food (natural wild foods that are collected or harvested) in Nunavut because harvested wild animals still make up so much of their diet. To date, all of the monitoring has shown that birds in Nunavut are safe and healthy for people to eat. However, there is evidence that some birds experience sub-lethal, or minor, negative health effects from contaminants in the Arctic environment, and disturbingly, the levels of some contaminants like mercury are increasing in birds in Nunavut. There is also an increase in garbage pollution, especially plastic, found on our land and in our waters, and some birds like northern fulmars mistake bits of plastic for food. Finally, some birds, like migrating ducks and seabirds, can become polluted or killed by environmental catastrophes, such as oil spills, that happen outside of Nunavut.

Harvest:

Some birds that nest in Nunavut are harvested not only here, but in other countries, too. Birds are harvested for their meat and their skins.

We can do something about all of these threats to reduce the chances of negative effects on birds. People must learn and practice ways to use less fossil fuel, to conserve energy, and to reduce greenhouse gases that feed global warming. We all should practice the three "R's"—reduce, reuse, and recycle—to minimize the garbage production that ends up polluting our environment. These are practical and achievable changes in behaviour that all Canadians need to make part of their daily life choices, if we are to see the threats of climate change and pollution reduced. As well, continued monitoring and open cooperation between countries regarding bird harvest will ensure long-term, sustainable harvest for people in and out of Nunavut.

Threats from development and shipping are handled through legal processes established in Canada to ensure that effects on wildlife are considered, avoided, or mitigated. Nonetheless, it is our responsibility to be vigilant and ensure that these processes are followed and improved where possible.

Some Nunavut Bird Trivia

Below are a few trivia questions on Nunavut birds that commonly get asked by students and tourists. The answers refer to birds that we expect to breed in Nunavut, and exclude those species that are really southern species but whose range sneaks north across the border, as well as accidental or vagrant species.

Which is the tallest species?

The sandhill crane stands tallest of the Nunavut birds at 120 centimetres.

Which is the smallest species?

The redpolls, either common or hoary, weigh between 11 and 20 grams.

What bird has the broadest wingspan?

The golden eagle (*Aquila chrysaetos*) wins this category with a wingspan of up to 234 centimetres.

Which is the heaviest species?

The tundra swan may weigh as much as 10 kilograms, heavier than the common loon, which can reach 7.6 kilograms.

Which bird can be found farthest north?

Northern fulmars, snow buntings, and black-legged kittiwakes have all been spotted close to the North Pole. In the winter, common ravens, snowy owls, and rock ptarmigan can all be found on Ellesmere Island.

Which bird has the longest migration?

The easy winner here is the Arctic tern, with some birds travelling more than 80,000 kilometres each year (that's twice around the Earth).

How many birds are there in Nunavut?

This is very difficult to answer, because we have poor or no estimates of the population size of many species, and we don't always know what percentage of a population breeds in Nunavut. However, coarse calculations suggest surprising similarities between groups. As a very rough estimate, in the Canadian Arctic in the summer there are probably close to 10 million shorebirds, at least 20 million landbirds, 10 million seabirds—if we include dovekies (*Alle alle*) that migrate through or feed in Nunavut—and 10 million waterfowl, for a total of 50 million birds. This is probably an underestimate.

Which species is the most abundant?

In some years, more than 10 million dovekies may be found in Nunavut waters in Baffin Bay, but these birds breed in Greenland. If we just consider the North American Arctic, there are estimates of up to 40 million Lapland longspurs (*Calcarius lapponicus*), 7 million snow geese, 3.5 million semipalmated sandpipers (*Calidris pusilla*), and 4.5 million thick-billed murres.

PHOTO: MARK MALLORY

What is the rarest breeding bird species?

Excluding those southern species whose breeding ranges just sneak into Nunavut, probably the rarest bird breeding in Nunavut is the Ross's gull, as we only know of four spots where they nest, and we cannot find more than ten nests in any given year.

Which bird species holds the most importance to Inuit?

The answer to this question varies depending on where you are in Nunavut. Different geese continue to be important components of Inuit diets, particularly in central and western Nunavut. In eastern Nunavut, the common eider is probably the bird most relied on by Inuit. Adults and eggs are consumed, and down is used for clothing.

PHOTO: MARK MALLORY

Where to See Birds in Nunavut

One can go anywhere in Nunavut and see birds, as they are distributed across the territory. Depending on what birds you want to see, there are some locations that provide higher chances of seeing certain types of birds. If you try this in winter, though, you probably won't see too many!

You are likely to see more birds by taking an Arctic cruise than by travelling on land, because you cover a much larger area in a ship, and have access to both terrestrial and marine bird species. Of course, the cruises are limited to the more ice-free season (generally from August through early October), and by this time most of the shorebirds have already headed south, so if they are your targets, you should consider land-based tours earlier in the season.

If you're interested in seeing marine birds, it's pretty tough to beat Pond Inlet, especially in the spring when so many of these birds frequent the floe edge, and outfitters and tour guides in the community offer trips to see the landscapes (where you can also see migrating marine mammals). Murres, fulmars, kittiwakes, guillemots, dovekies, gulls, eiders, jaegers, phalaropes, and long-tailed ducks (*Clangula hyemalis*) can all be spotted there. In May or June, thousands of snow geese head to nearby Bylot Island and can be seen flying near the community. The breeding colony at Cape Graham Moore has murres, kittiwakes, and glaucous gulls (*Larus hyperboreus*) on their nests by July. Many of these same species can also be spotted near Resolute Bay in the summer, but in smaller numbers.

If you are more interested in waterfowl and shorebirds, you should visit the community of Cambridge Bay on Victoria Island. Close to the community you can see nesting king eiders (*Somateria spectabilis*) and long-tailed ducks, as well as red-throated loons (*Gavia stellata*), phalaropes, and other shorebirds. A trip out with local guides may turn up Ross's geese, snow geese, tundra swans (*Cygnus columbianus*), and greater white-fronted geese (*Anser albifrons*).

A visit to Arviat will also allow you to see several types of Arctic waterfowl, loons, and shorebirds, and perhaps some species that are more common in the south, but may be creeping into Nunavut as the climate here becomes warmer, such as robins, swallows, sparrows, and ducks.

For die-hard birders looking to add some uncommon Arctic species to their lists, the most likely places to see ivory gulls (*Pagophila eburnea*) are Pond Inlet in the spring or Resolute Bay in late August or early September. Northern wheatears (*Oenanthe oenanthe*) are another target for many birders, and they are common around Iqaluit. Ross's gulls are rare and thus are a very unlikely bird to spot anywhere, but they have been seen flying near Arviat and Pond Inlet . . . although Siberia is a much easier place to spot them!

How to Use This Book

The following sections of the book describe some of the more common bird species that you may encounter if you travel to Nunavut. It is not intended to be a comprehensive field guide to all of the birds of Nunavut—there are plenty of those available in bookstores. Instead, the book highlights the most common, most threatened, or most interesting (in the author's opinion!) species found in the territory. Each species account provides the English, French, and Inuktitut names where possible; a brief description of the bird, where it occurs in Nunavut, and what it eats; a description of its habitat, nest, eggs, and behaviours; and some information (where available) on research on the species, its survival and population status, and local ecological knowledge about the bird. Finally, all species accounts include an interesting fact in the "Did You Know?" section.

The order of the species accounts follows the standard taxonomy of the bird families outlined earlier, and each account includes the following sections:

Marine – these birds are most likely to be seen on or near the ocean

Coastal – these birds are most likely to be seen along coastlines

Terrestrial – these birds are most likely to be seen inland on the tundra

FAMILY

Bird's Name

NAME
The names of the bird in English, French, Inuktitut (if available), and the scientific name in Latin.

APPEARANCE

A description of what the bird looks like at the time of year that people would see it in Nunavut (as many birds change their feathers and appear different in the winter). It starts by identifying whether the male and female have similar (monomorphic) or different (dimorphic) feather appearances, or whether the species has several forms (polymorphic). Sometimes the sexes are different in size but not appearance, and thus have been considered monomorphic. Where possible, the key distinguishing features that might help you identify the species are also noted.

RANGE

A map and description to help you learn where you might find this bird in Nunavut.

HABITAT

The environment where you are most likely to find this bird, along with some key survival needs of the bird, if known.

DIET

What the bird usually eats during its time in Nunavut.

REPRODUCTION

The normal number of eggs that the bird lays, what its nest looks like, and where you would find that nest.

BEHAVIOUR

Key actions or activities of the bird that might help you identify it at different times of the year.

RESEARCH AND MONITORING

What types of studies have been conducted on the species in Nunavut, and where those studies occurred.

SURVIVAL AND STATUS

Typical predators, population size, and changes in the species' numbers, and what we think the future holds for the species.

LOCAL ECOLOGICAL KNOWLEDGE

Particular aspects of a species that are known to Inuit through local ecological knowledge.

DID YOU KNOW?

If a bird species has a particularly extraordinary behaviour or an unusual characteristic, it'll be in this section.

PHOTO: MARK MALLORY

FAMILY GAVIIDAE

Red-throated Loon

INUKTITUT NAME
Qarsaaq; qaqsauq

FRENCH NAME
Plongeon catmarin; huard à gorge rousse

SCIENTIFIC NAME
Gavia stellata

APPEARANCE

Monomorphic. This loon is a relatively large seabird, longer than most ducks, but it is the smallest and least robust of the loons. The male is larger than the female, and an adult bird can weigh between 1.0 and 2.7 kilograms and have a wingspan of 110 centimetres. Its pale grey head and neck with distinctive, chestnut-red throat patch distinguish the adult bird. It has black-and-white speckling around its lower neck, back, and wings, and has a brownish to greyish-black tail with small white spots and slashes. The underside, or belly, is greyish white. A key feature to look for is its dark grey or black bill, which is relatively thin and tilted slightly upwards. Its webbed feet are dark grey to black.

Breeding Only

RANGE

The red-throated loon is one of our most widely distributed species, and can be found across all of Nunavut.

HABITAT

This loon nests in low wetlands, bogs, and ponds. Unlike other loons, this species can take off in a very short distance, and thus can nest on small water bodies (ponds generally less than 1.5 hectares). Most nest sites are within a few kilometres of the marine coastline, and ponds with one or more tiny islands are usually chosen for nest sites. During the breeding season, adults usually fly from their nest sites to the ocean to forage. The red-throated loon spends the winter at sea over sandy substrates along the eastern and western coasts of North America.

DIET

Carnivore. Red-throated loons are predators and primarily consume marine fish, but they also feed marine invertebrates to their chicks. They will sometimes feed in freshwater.

REPRODUCTION

Loon pairs defend small pond territories and thus nest individually. Their nests are always within a few metres of the water's edge, on low ground, and are usually built from a pile of aquatic vegetation. Females lay two glossy-brown or olive eggs with brown spots, and both the male and female share incubation and chick-rearing duties.

PHOTO: MARK MALLORY

BEHAVIOUR

Red-throated loons are found in pairs during the breeding season, but they may form groups of tens to hundreds during the winter. Like most loons, the red-throated loon runs to take off from the water—although this can be a very short distance—and in some instances, it can jump into the air directly from land. It slides on its belly when it lands back on a pond, like a plane landing on a runway. Its call is described as a "mournful wail," which is loud, weird, haunting, and unmistakable, and which can carry for great distances.

RESEARCH AND MONITORING

Loon populations have been monitored during waterfowl surveys in western Nunavut.

SURVIVAL AND STATUS

This loon is locally common, particularly in coastal wetland regions. Foxes and falcons may be important predators, while other birds (gulls, jaegers) may eat their eggs or chicks. The population size and trends for red-throated loons are largely unknown, although possibly declining.

LOCAL ECOLOGICAL KNOWLEDGE

Loon skins were used to make bags in which Inuit women stored *ivalu* (caribou or whale sinew thread), as well as Arctic cotton or dried moss for starting fires.

PHOTO: MARK MALLORY

DID YOU KNOW?

Loons are one of the oldest known types of living birds. There are fossilized loons from 25 million years ago!

FAMILY GAVIIDAE
Pacific Loon

INUKTITUT NAME
Marliq; kaglulik

FRENCH NAME
Plongeon de pacifique

SCIENTIFIC NAME
Gavia pacifica

APPEARANCE

Monomorphic. This loon is a relatively large seabird that weighs 1.2 to 2.5 kilograms and has a wingspan of 130 centimetres, the males being slightly larger than the females. This smooth-looking bird has a silvery-grey head, and black on the chin and throat to the breast. It has a small band of white stripes separating the chin from the neck, and a series of vertical white stripes on both sides of the neck, separating the black from the silvery-grey on the nape. Its breast and belly are bright white, while its back and tail are black. On its back, the Pacific loon has a series of small to large white patterned spots. Its black bill is short for a loon and is held horizontally. It has distinctive red eyes.

Breeding

RANGE

The Pacific loon is found across most of Nunavut south of 74°N. While some breed at Truelove Lowland on Devon Island, none are known to occur on the mountainous, northeastern part of Baffin Island. They winter in the ocean along the Pacific coast of North America.

HABITAT

This loon nests in freshwater lakes and ponds in low, flat, wet tundra, generally requiring less vegetation than the red-throated loon. It spends the winter near large bays, estuaries, and ocean shores.

DIET

Carnivore. Pacific loons are predators and primarily consume marine fish, but they also feed on aquatic invertebrates and crustaceans taken from both freshwater and saltwater.

REPRODUCTION

Loon pairs defend territories on their pond or lake. Their nests are always within a few metres of the water's edge, on low ground, and are usually built from piles of aquatic vegetation. Females lay two glossy-brown or olive eggs with brown spots, and both the male and female share incubation and chick-rearing duties.

BEHAVIOUR

Loon feet are very far back on the body, to help propel them in the water, but consequently loons move very awkwardly on land. Thus, they must nest close to water on flat ground. They also run across the water to take flight, requiring 30 to 50 metres of water to get airborne. Pacific loons are generally solitary or paired during breeding and often during the winter. They may occasionally be quite gregarious, flocking together in the thousands during migration.

RESEARCH AND MONITORING

Loon populations have been studied near Arviat, and Pacific loons are monitored during waterfowl and shorebird surveys in parts of Nunavut.

SURVIVAL AND STATUS

This loon is locally common, particularly in coastal wetland regions. There are few reports of predation on adult loons, but foxes, falcons, gulls, and jaegers may be important predators of eggs and chicks. The population size for Pacific loons is more than 400,000 birds, but numbers in Nunavut are unknown. Their populations have shifted in some locations, but overall appear to be stable.

LOCAL ECOLOGICAL KNOWLEDGE

Loon skins were used to make bags in which Inuit women stored *ivalu* (caribou or whale sinew thread), as well as Arctic cotton or dried moss for starting fires.

DID YOU KNOW?
During their first three weeks of life, loon chicks sometimes ride on their parents' backs.

PHOTO: JIM RICHARDS

PHOTO: JIM RICHARDS

FAMILY GAVIIDAE
Yellow-billed Loon

INUKTITUT NAME
Tuulligjuaq

FRENCH NAME
Plongeon à bec blanc

SCIENTIFIC NAME
Gavia adamsii

APPEARANCE

Monomorphic. This species in the largest loon in North America, with a mass of four to six kilograms (the females are heavier than the males) and a wingspan of 150 centimetres. This bird has a long, low profile in the water (unlike waterfowl, which appear to be floating on top of the water), and appears large. During the breeding season, it is blackish on its neck, back, and tail—with extensive white spotting or checkering on its back—and all white on the breast, belly, and undertail. It has a distinctive patch of vertical white stripes (called a necklace) at the base of its neck. The head, neck, and throat appear black, although up close they have a purplish sheen. The eyes are a distinctive red, and the underwings are white. In flight, the head is held low and the black webbed feet trail behind. A key feature to look for is its large, long, pale yellow bill.

RANGE

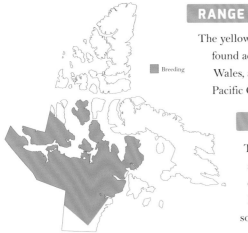

Breeding

The yellow-billed loon is a bird of central and western Nunavut, found across all of the mainland, as well as Victoria, Prince of Wales, and King William Islands. It spends the winter in the Pacific Ocean along the coast of Alaska and British Columbia.

HABITAT

This loon nests in flat, low tundra regions with lakes and slow-moving rivers. It nests on islands or shorelines of large freshwater lakes, generally larger than eight hectares. It winters on the marine coastline, but also in some inland lakes.

DIET

Carnivore. Loons primarily consume both freshwater and saltwater fish, but they also catch marine invertebrates to feed their chicks. This species sometimes consumes vegetation.

REPRODUCTION

Loon pairs vigorously defend their breeding territories. They nest within a few metres of the water's edge, on low ground. Their nests are usually piles of mud and aquatic vegetation, on which the females lay one to two olive-brown eggs with many dark brown splotches. Both the males and females take turns incubating the eggs, and feeding and rearing the chicks.

BEHAVIOUR

Yellow-billed loons are found in singles or pairs during the breeding season, and they may form groups of tens to hundreds during the winter. This loon runs to take off from the water, meaning that it cannot land on very small water bodies. It slides on its belly when it lands back on a pond, like a plane landing on a runway. Its call is a loud, mournful, harsh wail, although it also yodels and laughs.

RESEARCH AND MONITORING

Loon research has been conducted on Victoria Island, and loons are counted as part of regional waterfowl surveys in central Nunavut.

SURVIVAL AND STATUS

There are probably a few thousand pairs of this loon in Nunavut, but population trends are unknown.

LOCAL ECOLOGICAL KNOWLEDGE

Loon skins were used to make bags in which Inuit women stored *ivalu* (caribou or whale sinew thread), as well as Arctic cotton or dried moss for starting fires.

 DID YOU KNOW?
In some years, the ice on lakes and rivers melts too late in the year, preventing yellow-billed loons from breeding.

PHOTO: JIM RICHARDS

FAMILY PROCELLARIIDAE

Northern Fulmar

INUKTITUT NAME
Qaqulluk

FRENCH NAME
Fulmar boréal

SCIENTIFIC NAME
Fulmarus glacialis

APPEARANCE

Monomorphic. Many people who see fulmars think they are gulls, but they are quite different birds. Fulmars are the only petrels (seabirds with small tubes on top of their bills) in Nunavut. They are medium-sized, thick-necked, gull-like seabirds weighing 600 to 1,000 grams, with a wingspan of 110 centimetres, and are often seen gliding or soaring for several minutes without flapping their wings. Fulmars are highly variable in appearance. They can appear gull-like, with all-white heads and ventral surfaces and grey backs and wings, or they can be completely grey. In Nunavut, the most common form is a moderately grey bird with a light underbelly (darker overall than a gull). The yellow-green-grey fulmar bill has a distinctive tube on top.

RANGE

Breeding

In Nunavut, fulmars breed in 11 colonies in the High Arctic and eastern Baffin Island, and they can be found anywhere in the marine zone in Baffin Bay and Davis Strait, Lancaster Sound, Jones Sound, and in the northern portions of Prince Regent Inlet and Peel Sound, generally north of Bellot Strait. Some birds enter Hudson Strait, but are absent in any significant numbers from Hudson Bay and Foxe Basin. In the winter, most birds reside in the Labrador Sea or east of Newfoundland and Labrador, but some may migrate to European waters.

HABITAT

Fulmars principally breed in the High Arctic, with some colonies as far south as Qikiqtarjuaq, nesting on ledges of steep cliffs overlooking the ocean, as well as on top of broad rock stacks up to 500 metres high. These birds are commonly observed at sea, generally in the pelagic zone up to 500 kilometres from their breeding colonies.

DIET

Carnivore and scavenger. Fulmars eat squid, zooplankton, jellyfish, and fish (especially Arctic cod), and will also scavenge marine mammal carcasses. Fulmars are renowned for following fishing vessels, and scavenging bait and discarded bits of butchered fish. They are principally surface feeders, although they can dive up to three metres.

REPRODUCTION

Fulmars typically nest in colonies with thousands of other fulmars. The fulmar's nest is simply a scrape in the dirt or in a rock ledge, on which they lay one whitish egg. If she loses that egg, the female fulmar does not lay a replacement. Male and female fulmars share incubation and chick-rearing duties.

PHOTO: MARK MALLORY

BEHAVIOUR

Fulmars can be distinguished from gulls because they hold their wings stiffly and stroke their wings rapidly before soaring, whereas gulls typically bend their wings and beat them more slowly. Fulmars often glide effortlessly just above the water surface, the tips of their wings touching the tops of the waves. They are virtually silent when away from their breeding colonies, and they often follow boats (especially fishing boats), looking for bits of fish or bait that may be thrown overboard. They can projectile vomit fish oil stored in their throats to defend themselves against predators, other fulmars, Inuit egg hunters, or seabird biologists.

PHOTO: MARK MALLORY

PHOTO: MARK MALLORY

RESEARCH AND MONITORING

A major study on fulmar breeding and habitat use was conducted at Cape Vera, on Devon Island, and fulmar reproductive success and diet has been monitored on Prince Leopold Island and elsewhere in Lancaster Sound. Fulmar eggs have been studied since 1975 as indicators of contamination levels in the marine environment.

SURVIVAL AND STATUS

The northern fulmar is a common seabird, mostly in the Qikiqtani region. There are about 500,000 fulmars in Nunavut, and their population appears to be in slow decline; there were probably more fulmars in Nunavut in the past. Fulmars may live for more than 50 years. Arctic foxes, common ravens, and glaucous gulls eat fulmar eggs or chicks, while falcons and foxes may kill adults.

PHOTO: MARK MALLORY

LOCAL ECOLOGICAL KNOWLEDGE

The northern fulmar plays a major role in the Inuit legend of Sedna, the sea goddess, and the most powerful being in Inuit mythology. In some versions of the legend, it was the fulmar that disguised itself as a man to become her husband and take her to his home. When Sedna's father came to her rescue, the fulmar used its powerful wings to create a storm to stop them. The father threw Sedna overboard and cut her fingers off when she tried to climb back in the boat, and these fingers became the creatures of the sea.

PHOTO: MARK MALLORY

DID YOU KNOW?

Northern fulmars are one of three bird species that have been observed very close to the North Pole. The fulmar also has the dubious distinction of being the first wildlife species in Nunavut in which scientists have found plastic garbage—fulmars mistake bits of garbage floating in the ocean as food and eat them.

Tundra Swan

INUKTITUT NAME
Qugjuq

FRENCH NAME
Cygne siffleur

SCIENTIFIC NAME
Cygnus columbianus

PHOTO: JIM RICHARDS

APPEARANCE

Monomorphic. Adult tundra swans are large, unmistakable white birds with very long, distinctive necks. Juvenile birds have dullish grey feathers. They are the only swans found in Nunavut. They usually weigh between 5.6 and 7.2 kilograms, and the males may be a bit larger than the females. They have large wingspans of up to 220 centimetres, and a powerful, slow, rhythmic flight. Their feet, legs, and bills are black, although the bills on juveniles may be dirty pink.

Breeding Only

RANGE

Swans breed in the Low and High Arctic, but are most common between 66°N and 70°N. Breeding swans can be found on southern Baffin Island and around the coast of Hudson Bay, but the densest concentrations of birds are on the barren lands of the northern Kivalliq and Kitikmeot regions. In the winter, swans are found on the east and west coasts of the United States.

HABITAT

This is a bird of the broad, wet, flat tundra. They nest on the tundra along low coasts or inland areas with low relief and many small ponds, wetlands, and lakes. Feeding is principally in freshwater wetlands and ponds.

DIET

Herbivore. Swans eat submergent aquatic plants, although they may also graze on some terrestrial vegetation, and during migration and wintering they will eat grain. They also consume mollusks.

REPRODUCTION

Swans are territorial during the breeding season. In the right habitats, swans may nest as densely as two pairs per square kilometre, but usually they are more dispersed. Their nests are on top of mounds built from dead aquatic vegetation. They lay two to five creamy-white eggs, and the male and female share incubation and chick-rearing duties.

BEHAVIOUR

Swans mate for life, and migrate south with their families. During migration and in the winter, swans are gregarious, travelling in flocks of up to 100 individuals, but they are distinctly aggressive towards other swans or potential predators during the breeding season. After the eggs hatch, swan families often move from their smaller nesting ponds to larger lakes or rivers, where adults replace some of their flight feathers before migration.

RESEARCH AND MONITORING

Swan populations have been monitored during waterfowl surveys on western Baffin Island and central and western Nunavut.

SURVIVAL AND STATUS

The tundra swan is a common bird, mostly in central and western Nunavut. There are about 150,000 tundra swans in North America, mostly from Nunavut, and that population is considered to be stable. They defend their nests well, but foxes may still get their eggs.

PHOTO: CREDENCE WOOD

DID YOU KNOW?

Tundra swans were once called whistling swans because of the noise made by their wings.

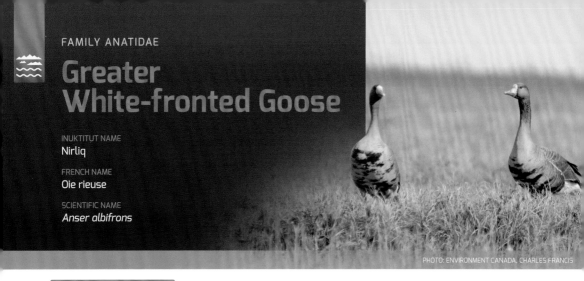

FAMILY ANATIDAE

Greater White-fronted Goose

INUKTITUT NAME
Nirliq

FRENCH NAME
Oie rieuse

SCIENTIFIC NAME
Anser albifrons

APPEARANCE

Monomorphic. This medium-sized goose weighs two to three kilograms, the male being larger than the female. Its wingspan extends to 160 centimetres. It is dark, with a dark grey-brown head, neck, wings, back, and tail. It has black barring or spotting on its chest. It has white feathers on its belly and under its tail, as well as distinctive white feathers between its bill and eyes. Its bill is pink and its legs are orange.

Breeding

RANGE

White-fronted geese breed in central and western Nunavut on the mainland (Kent Peninsula, Queen Maud Gulf lowlands, Boothia Peninsula), as well as on southern Victoria Island and King William Island. They migrate through the Canadian prairies and spend the winter along the coast of the Gulf of Mexico, as well as in the highlands of Mexico.

HABITAT

Breeding sites for these geese are lowland Arctic tundra; swampy areas, lakes, and ponds; areas dominated by vegetation, including sedges, grasses, and mosses; and upland hummocky areas. They move with their young to stream and lake edges with nearby grass-sedge meadows, where they can escape predators and feed and rear their young. In the winter they feed along coastal wetlands as well as agricultural areas.

DIET

Herbivore. Greater white-fronted geese eat grasses, sedges, berries, and parts of aquatic plants year-round, although in the winter, they feed largely on waste grain in agricultural fields.

REPRODUCTION

This goose tends to nest solitarily or in loose aggregations, not true colonies, and defends a territory near its nest. The nest may be a scrape in the ground or a mound of mud and vegetation, and is lined with downy feathers. The female usually lays four to five creamy-white eggs, and then undertakes incubation while the male defends her and the nest. Both parents participate in rearing the goslings.

BEHAVIOUR

Greater white-fronted geese tend to mate for life, and maintain family groups into the next breeding season. Yearling (immature) geese may act as sentinels to alert their nesting parents to predators nearby, and they may even defend their parents' nests.

RESEARCH AND MONITORING

Long-term studies of the breeding success and population size of white-fronted geese have been conducted in the Queen Maud Gulf Migratory Bird Sanctuary.

SURVIVAL AND STATUS

The portion of the greater white-fronted goose population that breeds in Nunavut is probably between 600,000 and 1 million birds. These birds are in decline early in the twenty-first century, which is a concern for wildlife managers. Only a few hundred of these geese are harvested by Inuit, but foxes, gulls, ravens, and occasionally wolverines and bears may depredate their nests.

PHOTO: JIM LEAFLOOR

PHOTO: JIM RICHARDS

DID YOU KNOW?

This goose and its close relatives are the most widespread type of goose in the northern hemisphere. As well, this goose travels farther south for the winter than any other Arctic-nesting goose.

FAMILY ANATIDAE

Snow Goose

INUKTITUT NAME
Kanguq

FRENCH NAME
Oie des neiges; oie blanche

SCIENTIFIC NAME
Chen caerulescens

APPEARANCE

Snow geese occur in two colour morphs, but males and females can be either white (light morph) or blue (dark morph). This medium-sized goose weighs 1.7 to 3.3 kilograms, the males being larger than the females. Its wingspan extends to 170 centimetres. The more common light morph has all-white plumage, except for black primary feathers. The feathers on the head are often stained a rusty orange. The less common dark morph is referred to as the blue goose and has a variable colour pattern, typically a dark grey-brown body with a white head and foreneck and a dark brownish-grey underside. The upper wing is grey, the rump is pale grey, and the upper tail is grey or white, but the main feathers of the tail are dark grey. In adults of both colour morphs, the legs and bill are pinkish, and the bill has a distinctive black grinning patch.

RANGE

Snow geese breed in colonies scattered around the Low and High Arctic. Major colonies occur along western Hudson Bay, Southampton Island, southwestern Baffin Island, Bylot Island, and Queen Maud Gulf (many of these are migratory bird sanctuaries). Smaller colonies or pairs of birds breed as far as northern Ellesmere Island. In the winter, geese inhabit estuaries, marine bays, and coastal prairies of the southeastern, central, and western United States.

Breeding

HABITAT

In the Low Arctic, snow geese are usually found in flat, wet, coastal tundra areas, nesting in coastal and salt marshes, ponds, shallow lakes, streams, and braided river deltas. In the High Arctic, snow geese can also be found nesting inland on rolling terrain or vegetated, polygon formations. After hatching, geese move towards ponds and lakes, feeding on the surrounding vegetation. They moult along the shores of inland lakes where they can escape predation.

DIET

Herbivore. Snow geese eat grasses, sedges, rushes, and parts of aquatic plants. In the winter, they feed largely on waste grain in agricultural fields.

PHOTO: NADINE LAMOUREAUX

REPRODUCTION

Snow geese nest in colonies but maintain small territories near their nests. Nest density can be high (700 per square kilometre), although this is unusual. The female builds the nest, which may be a scrape in the ground or on a mound, and lines it with down and vegetation. The female usually lays three to five creamy-white eggs, and the male and female share incubation and gosling rearing.

BEHAVIOUR

Snow geese mate for life and migrate south with their families. They are gregarious all through the year, sometimes occurring in flocks of tens of thousands in the winter, and nesting in colonies of hundreds of thousands. Geese are highly aggressive towards other animals approaching their nests. Once the eggs hatch, goose families form groups and move to larger ponds and lakes.

RESEARCH AND MONITORING

Long-term studies of snow geese (breeding biology, behaviour, genetics, ecology) have been conducted on western Baffin Island, Bylot Island, Southampton Island, western Hudson Bay, and near the Queen Maud Gulf.

SURVIVAL AND STATUS

The North American snow goose population has increased dramatically since the 1950s due to stricter hunting regulations, changes in agricultural practices in the migration and wintering areas, and the establishment of refuges and bird sanctuaries. Early in the twenty-first century, we estimate that there are 4 to 7 million geese, 80% of which are probably in Nunavut. Snow geese may live more than 26 years. In an average year, Inuit eat 12,000 snow geese and 15,000 of their eggs. Arctic foxes are key predators of snow geese, eating their eggs and young, but gulls, ravens, jaegers, wolves, wolverine, and bears may also destroy their nests.

DID YOU KNOW?

Numbers of snow geese in Low Arctic colonies have become so high that they are destroying tundra by overgrazing the vegetation, including eating the plants' roots. The areas destroyed by geese are large enough to be detected by satellites. To help minimize the damage, a special spring hunting season was enacted in the United States and Canada to try to reduce goose numbers. To date, this has had limited success.

FAMILY ANATIDAE
Ross's Goose

INUKTITUT NAME
Qaaraarjuk

FRENCH NAME
Oie de Ross

SCIENTIFIC NAME
Chen rossii

APPEARANCE

Ross's geese occur in two colour morphs, but males and females can be either white (light morph) or blue (dark morph). This small goose weighs one to two kilograms (smaller than some ducks) and has a 110-centimetre wingspan. The males are larger than the females. The much more common light morph has all-white plumage, except for black primary feathers. The less common dark morph has a variable colour pattern, typically a dark grey-brown body with a white head, foreneck, rump, and tail. In all adults, the legs and bill are pinkish. Aside from being smaller, the bill of the Ross's goose does not have the black grinning patch found on snow geese.

Breeding

RANGE

Over 90% of all Ross's geese breed in the Queen Maud Gulf Migratory Bird Sanctuary in central Nunavut, although the species is expanding its range eastward along western Hudson Bay, Southampton Island, and western Baffin Island. It is found in northern California, northern Mexico, the south-central United States, and the Gulf of Mexico coast in the winter.

HABITAT

Ross's geese are usually found on sparsely vegetated islands and surrounding flat, wet tundra near shallow Arctic lakes, as well as some riverine and offshore islands. They moult along the shores of inland lakes where they can escape predation. Their winter habitats include agricultural fields and shallow wetlands.

DIET

Herbivore. Ross's geese eat grasses, sedges, and various seeds, and in the winter, waste grain in agricultural fields.

REPRODUCTION

Ross's geese nest in colonies but maintain small territories near their nests. Nest density on islands can be high (more than 1,000 per square kilometre), although on mainland nesting areas the number is usually lower. The nest is a scrape in the ground or a small mound of vegetation lined with down. The female lays two to nine (usually four) creamy-white eggs, and she incubates while the male guards her and the nest. Both parents help rear the goslings.

BEHAVIOUR

Ross's geese are highly gregarious all through the year, migrating in large flocks (sometimes up to hundreds of thousands in the winter) and nesting in high densities. Like all geese, they can be highly aggressive towards other geese or animals approaching their nests.

PHOTO: DANA KELLETT

RESEARCH AND MONITORING

Long-term studies of Ross's geese (breeding biology, behaviour, ecology) have been conducted in the Queen Maud Gulf Migratory Bird Sanctuary.

SURVIVAL AND STATUS

Estimates from 2001 suggest that there were approximately 1 million Ross's geese, and their population was still increasing dramatically. Ross's geese are hunted in North America, and Inuit from many communities also harvest Ross's geese and their eggs. Wild Ross's geese may live more than 20 years. Arctic foxes are a key predator of their eggs and young, but gulls, ravens, jaegers, wolves, wolverine, and bears may also destroy their nests.

DID YOU KNOW?

The Ross's goose was considered the rarest of North American geese early in the twentieth century, with less than 5,000 birds counted. That changed dramatically with new sport hunting restrictions and the development of protected areas for this species where it breeds, migrates, and spends the winter. However, like snow geese, scientists now believe that the population of Ross's geese is too high.

Brant

INUKTITUT NAME
Nirlinnaq

FRENCH NAME
Bernache cravant

SCIENTIFIC NAME
Branta bernicla (subspecies *bernicla, hrota, nigricans*)

PHOTO:MARK MALLORY

APPEARANCE

Monomorphic. Brant are small, dark geese that weigh 1.2 to 1.8 kilograms—with males larger than females—and have wingspans of 120 centimetres. The feathers on their heads, necks, breasts, tails, and legs are black, as well as the primary feathers on their wings. Their belly feathers are variable, ranging from grey to dark grey to black, and their sides and backs are grey to brown. The undersides of their tails are white. They have small, variable patterns of white striations (stripes) in the middles of their necks, which are distinctive and can be used to identify individuals.

RANGE

Breeding

Brant have a widespread breeding distribution from the Low to High Arctic. In the Low Arctic, brant tend to nest in colonies, whereas in the High Arctic they breed in more dispersed areas. They can be found nesting along western Hudson Bay, all of Foxe Basin, Southampton Island, western Baffin Island, and all of the High Arctic Archipelago to northern Ellesmere Island. In the winter, brant are found on mudflats and shallow marine bays supporting eelgrass. Different subpopulations in Nunavut migrate to distinctly different wintering areas. Brant from the western Arctic migrate to the Pacific coast of Canada and the United States south to Baja, California, while those from Foxe Basin migrate to the Atlantic coast of the United States south to North Carolina, and the High Arctic brant migrate east to Iceland and then Ireland for the winter.

HABITAT

In the Low Arctic, brant usually inhabit salt marshes and estuarine deltas with grassy vegetation, and in particular they are noted for nesting on islands and gravel spits in rivers. In the High Arctic, they tend to be found up to 30 kilometres inland along braided rivers, deltas, and lakes. After hatching, families move to coastal areas less than one kilometre from tidal areas, as well as mossy shorelines of lakes and rocky offshore islands. Like other geese, adults tend to moult along the shores of inland lakes where they can escape predation.

DIET

Herbivore. Brant eat grasses, some leafy plants, and occasionally mosses, eelgrass, and some mollusks. In the winter, they rely heavily on eelgrass and salt marsh plants.

REPRODUCTION

Brant nest in small colonies dispersed along coasts or river systems. The brant nest is typically a scrape in the ground or a depression in gravel, lined with brownish down. The female lays three to five creamy-white eggs. She incubates the eggs while the male guards her, but both the male and the female rear the goslings.

BEHAVIOUR

Like many geese, brant mate for life, and migrate south with their families. They are usually found in groups throughout the year, although more so in winter. Brant vigorously defend their nests against intruders. They lower and extend their necks in a threat posture and make hissing noises. When in flight, brant are remarkably agile for fairly large and stout birds, and can chase gulls and jaegers with great proficiency.

RESEARCH AND MONITORING

Brant studies have been undertaken on Southampton and Bathurst Islands, and brant are counted in waterfowl surveys across parts of Nunavut. Brant wintering in Ireland were equipped with satellite transmitters, and they travelled to High Arctic Canada, where one was shot by a hunter in Resolute Bay!

PHOTO: MARK MALLORY

SURVIVAL AND STATUS

The three subspecies of brant are thought to total 300,000 birds, but the population fluctuates dramatically from year to year. Brant are harvested by Inuit, but annual numbers taken are low. Brant eggs and young may be eaten by foxes, falcons, gulls, and jaegers.

DID YOU KNOW?

Many of the brant that migrate from Nunavut to Ireland for the winter stop over to eat and rest at Bessastadir, the presidential residence of Iceland, near Reykjavik.

FAMILY ANATIDAE

Canada Goose

INUKTITUT NAME
Nedlenuk; nirlik uluagullik

FRENCH NAME
Bernache du Canada

SCIENTIFIC NAME
Branta canadensis
(subspecies *canadensis, interior, maxima, moffitti, parvipes, occidentalis, fulva, hutchinsii, taverneri, minima, leucopareia*)

PHOTO: JIM LEAFLOOR

APPEARANCE

Monomorphic. This large, dark goose varies greatly in size, depending on the race in question. Some Canada geese are not much larger than ducks, while others weigh up to nine kilograms. In most cases, the males are larger than the females. This species is one of the most recognizable wild birds in Canada. The head and neck are black except for a conspicuous white chin stripe, the upper body is greyish brown, and the rump and tail are black, although the upper tail is white. The underside of the body is a lighter brownish grey, becoming white under the lower belly and tail. The bill and legs are black.

RANGE

Breeding

The Canada goose can be found breeding south of 70°N across all of mainland Nunavut, as well as southern Baffin Island, Southampton Island, and parts of Victoria Island. The range of this goose has been spreading farther north, notably to Baffin Island. In the winter this species is distributed broadly across parts of southern Canada and much of the southern and coastal areas of the United States.

HABITAT

These geese breed on vegetated coastal plains and inland meadows, typically areas of low relief near freshwater. In more mountainous areas (like Baffin Island), Canada geese are found nesting along vegetated valleys. They use similar habitats for moulting and breeding. In the winter, they are commonly found on coastal marshes and grasslands, reservoirs, and rivers near agricultural areas.

DIET

Herbivore. Canada geese principally consume grasses, sedges, rushes, aquatic plants, berries, seeds, and agricultural grains.

REPRODUCTION

These geese nest either individually or semi-colonially, and they are highly territorial around their nest sites. Their nests are often mounds of vegetation lined with downy feathers, in which four to six creamy-white eggs are laid. After hatching, the parents move their young to areas with freshwater ponds for safety, as the parents moult and are flightless for much of this period. Only the female incubates the eggs, but the male remains with the female through incubation and chick rearing.

PHOTO: CREDENCE WOOD

BEHAVIOUR

Canada geese mate for life, and they will defend their nests very vigorously against all intruders, including people. Canada geese are gregarious during migration and wintering. Their call is the distinctive "honking" most associated with geese, and they form the classic flocks that fly in "V" formations during their spring and fall migration.

RESEARCH AND MONITORING

Studies of Canada geese have been undertaken mostly in western Hudson Bay and Southampton Island, although surveys for this species have been conducted along many of the rivers of the Kivalliq and Kitikmeot regions.

SURVIVAL AND STATUS

The number of Canada geese in North America has increased dramatically since the 1940s.
Some races of geese have experienced declines, while other races, like the giant Canada goose, have exploited urban situations and grown in number. There are an estimated 5 million Canada geese in North America, although the number breeding in Nunavut is much smaller. More than 5,000 Canada geese are harvested annually in Nunavut by Inuit. In addition, eggs and goslings may be eaten by foxes, bears, ravens, gulls, and jaegers.

LOCAL ECOLOGICAL KNOWLEDGE

Interviews were used to show that the range of the Canada goose on Baffin Island has been moving northward. Inuit harvest eggs from goose nests located farther north than was known based on scientific surveys.

DID YOU KNOW?

In 2004, the races or subspecies of Canada geese were split into two groups, Canada geese and cackling geese. The cackling goose species, now known as *Branta hutchinsii*, can be distinguished with a little work—they are smaller, with relatively short necks and stubby bills, and are more commonly found in the West. This species includes the *minima*, *hutchinsii*, *taverneri*, and *leucopareia* groups.

King Eider

INUKTITUT NAME
Kingalik

FRENCH NAME
Eider à tête grise

SCIENTIFIC NAME
Somateria spectabilis

PHOTO: JIM RICHARDS

APPEARANCE

Dimorphic. The king eider is a large, robust diving duck that weighs 1.2 to 2.1 kilograms—slightly smaller than the common eider—and has a wingspan of about 94 centimetres. During the breeding season, females are a cryptic, mottled brown colour, and have long, dusky-green bills. They look similar to female common eiders, except that female king eiders are often darker and more reddish brown, and the dark bars on their feathers are shaped like a "V" more than a "C." The males are unmistakable and stunning. They have a large orange knob between the bill and forehead, pearl-blue feathers on the forehead and back of the neck, pale greenish cheek feathers, and an orange bill. The rest of the head, neck, and breast feathers are creamy white, while the remainder of the body feathers are black. In the winter, the males look similar to the females.

■ Breeding

RANGE

King eiders are widespread across the Low to High Arctic, from western Hudson Bay to the northern part of Ellesmere Island, making them one of the most northern nesting birds. Unlike common eiders, there is just one race of king eiders in Nunavut. The birds breeding from Queen Maud Gulf and Victoria Island migrate west to the coasts of Alaska and Russia for the winter, while the birds nesting east of Victoria Island migrate east to winter in Greenland or along the coast of Newfoundland and Labrador.

HABITAT

King eiders nest in low, marshy, vegetated habitats adjacent to freshwater lakes and ponds, or on small islands. They are not colonial. During the breeding season they forage in deeper water (up to 20 metres) than common eiders. In winter their range overlaps with that of common eiders, in shallow bays and rocky coasts or near ice edges.

DIET

Omnivore. King eiders dive for mollusks and benthic invertebrates, such as sea urchins, when feeding at sea, but during the breeding season they also feed on aquatic plants and insect larvae.

PHOTO: MARK MALLORY

REPRODUCTION

These ducks' nests are individually dispersed across the tundra. The nest is a scrape in the ground, lined with down and vegetation. Females lay three to six large, pale olive-green eggs. Only the female incubates; the male abandons the female during incubation and leaves the area to join other males in large rafts on the ocean, where they moult their flight feathers.

BEHAVIOUR

King eiders are gregarious in the winter, often forming flocks of thousands of birds, but are seen as individuals, pairs, or small groups during the breeding season. They can dive to depths of 55 metres to forage. King eiders often migrate with other species of eiders. Their migration passage, particularly in the western Arctic, is spectacular, and birds can continue to stream past a location for hours.

RESEARCH AND MONITORING

Breeding biology of king eiders has been studied intensively in Nunavut on the Kent Peninsula and in the Queen Maud Gulf Migratory Bird Sanctuary. Partnership research on migration ecology has also been conducted between scientists in Canada, the United States of America, and Greenland.

SURVIVAL AND STATUS

These eiders are broadly distributed and locally common in Nunavut, with an estimated 300,000 to 400,000 birds in the western population, and up to 250,000 birds in the eastern population. The overall population has declined since the 1970s. Adults, eggs, and down are harvested by Inuit in different communities in Nunavut. Eider eggs and young may be eaten by Arctic foxes and predatory birds, and adults may be killed by falcons and owls.

DID YOU KNOW?

During spring migration, king eiders form large groups in leads in the ice or polynyas, waiting for the snow to melt and lakes to thaw so they can move to their breeding grounds. If the spring melt is very late, or ice conditions suddenly change, thousands of eiders can die together due to starvation.

Common Eider

INUKTITUT NAME
Mitiq

FRENCH NAME
Eider à duvet

SCIENTIFIC NAME
Somateria mollissima
(subspecies *borealis, v-nigra, sedentaria*)

PHOTO: MARK MALLORY

APPEARANCE

Dimorphic. This large, robust diving duck, weighing 1.2 to 2.6 kilograms (which is heavier than some geese), is the largest duck in North America. A common eider's wingspan can reach 108 centimetres. During the breeding season, females are a cryptic, mottled brown, and have a long, dusky-green bill that extends up the front of the head towards their eyes (longer than other ducks). In contrast, males have dramatic, bright white feathers on their heads, necks, breasts, and backs, contrasted against their black tails, wingtips, sides of the body, and bellies. The top of the male's head has a black cap, and from the cheek to the back of the head, the male is pale green. The male's bill is variable but brighter than the female's, with yellow or orange colouration. During the winter, males develop a more cryptic plumage, closer to that of the females.

RANGE

Breeding

Winter

Common eiders are found across Nunavut, from James Bay to Ellesmere Island, although their population size is larger in the Low Arctic. The southernmost race in Nunavut is the *S. m. sedentaria* race, found in James and Hudson Bays north to Hudson Strait. Eiders breeding in Hudson Strait, around Baffin Island, and across the High Arctic are the *S. m. borealis* race; colonies in the Kitikmeot region of Nunavut near Victoria Island and Queen Maud Gulf are the *S. m. v-nigra* race. *S. m. v-nigra* migrate and winter in Alaska and eastern Russia. *S. m. borealis* migrate to waters along the west coast of Greenland, as well as Newfoundland and Labrador, and *S. m. sedentaria* remain in Hudson Bay all year.

HABITAT

Common eiders live around rocky marine coasts and islands in shallow waters (ten metres or less). Preferred nesting sites are small, low islands that lack mammalian predators, and have at least one freshwater pond. Common eiders forage along the intertidal zone and on mussel beds. In the winter, they may forage along the floe edge or in polynyas over mussel beds.

DIET

Carnivore. Eiders dive for mollusks and benthic invertebrates, such as sea urchins.

REPRODUCTION

Common eiders nest in colonies that range from a few birds to thousands of pairs, and nests can be within a few centimetres of one another. The nest is a scrape in the ground, lined with down and occasionally vegetation. The female typically lays four to eight eggs—nests with more than this number are the result of another female laying some eggs in the nest. Fewer eggs are laid if the female starts the nest late in the season, or if the bird nests farther north. Only the female incubates; the male abandons the female during incubation and leaves the area in order to moult his flight feathers.

PHOTO: MARK MALLORY

BEHAVIOUR

Common eiders are gregarious throughout the year, breeding colonially, migrating in flocks, and wintering together in large groups. During the fall and early winter, male and female eiders have similar feathers, but the males moult and grow their bright breeding plumage before they migrate to the colony. Female eiders and their broods form crèches such that large broods of eiders (50 chicks) might be attended by three or four females.

RESEARCH AND MONITORING

Breeding ecology, adult survival, wildlife health and factors influencing population status of eiders have been studied intensively in Nunavut on the Belcher Islands, on Southampton Island, near Devon Island, and around the Kent Peninsula in western Nunavut. Partnership research on migration ecology has been conducted between scientists in Canada, the United States of America, and Greenland.

SURVIVAL AND STATUS

Common eiders are broadly distributed and locally common in Nunavut, with a total population of around 800,000 birds. There are an estimated 400,000 to 500,000 birds in the *S. m. borealis* population, which is stable; 100,000 birds in the *S. m. v-nigra* population, which is in decline; and 200,000 birds in the *S. m. sedentaria* population, which has recovered from declines in the 1990s. Common eider adults, eggs, and down are harvested by many aboriginal communities in Nunavut, with approximately 6,000 adults and thousands of eggs being harvested per year. Arctic foxes are a key predator of eggs and young, but gulls, ravens, jaegers, and bears may also destroy nests, and adults may be killed by owls and falcons.

PHOTO: MARK MALLORY

LOCAL ECOLOGICAL KNOWLEDGE

Many studies have been conducted on Inuit ecological knowledge of eiders, especially in Hudson Bay. Inuit know that eiders are sensitive to disturbance, and they have observed that eiders move their colonies when they are harassed by polar bears (such as in Frobisher Bay). They also know that if Inuit only harvest some of the down from nests, the eiders will keep incubating, but if they harvest all of the down, the eiders will abandon their nests. Inuit knowledge in Hudson Strait, around Hudson Bay, and Foxe Basin also suggests that there are no oral records of massive eider die-offs in the area. This suggests that the recent mortality events in this area due to avian cholera are new and possibly related to global warming.

PHOTO: MARK MALLORY

 ### DID YOU KNOW?

Common eiders migrate by flying over oceans and along coastlines; they almost never fly over land. In contrast, king eiders take "shortcuts," flying over land between major bodies of water. Also, the *S. m. sedentaria* race of eiders never leaves Hudson Bay, and in years of very heavy, extensive ice cover (like 1992), tens of thousands of eiders may starve because ice covers the areas where they normally feed.

PHOTO: MARK MALLORY

Harlequin Duck

INUKTITUT NAME
Turngaviaq

FRENCH NAME
Arlequin plongeur

SCIENTIFIC NAME
Histrionicus histrionicus

PHOTO: MIKE MCEVOY

APPEARANCE

Dimorphic. Harlequins are small, round diving ducks that weigh 500 to 750 grams. Like most other ducks, females are cryptic during the breeding season, with dull, dark brown feathering on their heads and backs, lighter brown on their chests, and creamy white on their undersides. Females each have a white patch between their bill and their eyes, and a distinctive bright white ellipse between their eyes and the back of their head. Males are spectacular, with slate-blue feathers on their heads, chests, wings, backs, and bellies. This blue is broken up by bold white patches (often lined in black) on the neck, side, and wings, and a crescent between the bill and eye. The tops of their heads and their sides are chestnut brown. In both sexes, the bills are grey. The legs and feet are greyish, but are sometimes tinged with yellow. During the winter, males resemble females, only darker.

RANGE

Harlequin ducks are found on southern Baffin Island in areas near Cape Dorset, Kimmirut, Frobisher Bay, and into Cumberland Sound. Individuals have occasionally been observed near Qikiqtarjuaq and even as far north as Pond Inlet. Some birds that breed in Québec moult along coastal areas of eastern Hudson Bay, east of the Belcher Islands. It is unclear where birds from Nunavut go in the winter, but we think they migrate east to the coast of Greenland.

Breeding

HABITAT

This small sea duck is found along rapidly flowing, clear streams and rivers during the breeding season and along shallow, rocky coastlines in the winter. During spring migration they may be found in small groups along the floe edge.

DIET

Carnivore. Harlequin ducks dive for aquatic insects, crustaceans, mollusks, sea urchins, and occasionally small fish.

REPRODUCTION

Harlequin ducks nest solitarily along rocky rivers and streams, usually in cover (boulders, crevices, or bases of vegetation). The nest is a scrape in the ground, lined with down and occasionally vegetation. Females typically lay three to seven eggs. The female incubates the eggs and the male abandons her during incubation and leaves the area to moult his flight feathers.

BEHAVIOUR

Harlequin ducks are found in flocks during migration and in the winter, but are usually seen as singles, pairs, or in family groups during the breeding season. They are often observed diving in the turbulent white water of streams and picking larval insects off the bottom. They are highly agile in strong currents.

SURVIVAL AND STATUS

There are probably no more than a few hundred individual harlequin ducks breeding in Nunavut. The eastern population of this duck, which includes those breeding in Nunavut, is listed as being of special concern to the Committee on the Status of Endangered Wildlife in Canada (COSEWIC) under the federal *Species at Risk Act.*

LOCAL ECOLOGICAL KNOWLEDGE

Interviews around southern Baffin Island in the early 2000s confirmed for the first time in 70 years that harlequins still inhabited parts of Nunavut.

PHOTO: MARK MALLORY

PHOTO: MIKE MCEVOY

DID YOU KNOW?

Harlequin ducks are named for the striking and bizarre plumage of the male, which is thought to resemble the traditional Italian comedy or pantomime character, the harlequin, who performed tricks and wore costumes of multicoloured triangular patches.

FAMILY ANATIDAE

Long-tailed Duck

INUKTITUT NAME
Aa'aangiq; aggiarjuk

FRENCH NAME
Harelde kakawi

SCIENTIFIC NAME
Clangula hyemalis

PHOTO: MARK MALLORY

APPEARANCE

Dimorphic. This is a medium-sized, tapered diving duck that weighs 700 to 1,000 grams. Male ducks undergo three feather moults in a year, which is unique among waterfowl. Both sexes are generally whitish in the winter and darker in the summer. Males are unmistakable with their long, central, streaming tail feathers, and both sexes have very short bills. During the breeding season, males have black breasts, crowns, napes, and tail feathers. They have white sides and white masks on their faces, with mottled brown feathers on their backs. In the winter, males have pink bands around their dark bills, and bright white heads. The female's pattern resembles the male's, but they usually have lighter, browner feathers and lack the exceptionally long central tail feathers.

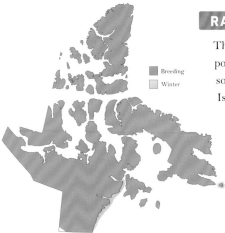

Breeding
Winter

RANGE

This bird is one of the most widespread in Nunavut, potentially found breeding anywhere near water from southern James Bay to the northern end of Ellesmere Island, and from eastern Baffin Island to the westernmost parts of the Kitikmeot region. Scientists still do not know where long-tailed ducks from different parts of Nunavut go in the winter, but it is known that some remain in polynyas near the Belcher Islands, while many nesting around Hudson Bay migrate to the Great Lakes, and those from the far North probably migrate either to Greenland, the Atlantic Coast, or waters off the coast of Alaska or Russia.

HABITAT

This duck is widespread across the Low and High Arctic. They are usually found along marine coastlines in shallow waters (less than nine metres). They nest in low, marshy, vegetated habitats adjacent to freshwater lakes and ponds, or on small islands. Although they may occur in high breeding densities, they are not considered colonial. During the breeding season, they forage in both freshwater and saltwater. They spend the winter in shallow coastal areas along the Pacific and Atlantic coasts, in the Great Lakes, and in large inland reservoirs.

DIET

Carnivore. Long-tailed ducks dive usually less than nine metres for small mollusks, crustaceans, and fish, but they also eat insects and worms during the breeding season. They can dive up to 60 metres, which is deeper than any other duck.

REPRODUCTION

Long-tailed ducks usually disperse their nests across the tundra, but in island situations, they may nest in association with Arctic terns, which protect them from predators. Long-tailed ducks typically lay six to eight cream-coloured eggs, but nests with eleven or more eggs have been found. These are the result of one or more females laying their eggs in another female's nest (brood parasitism). Only the female incubates the egg and rears the chicks; the male abandons the female during incubation and gathers with other males to moult.

BEHAVIOUR

Long-tailed ducks are relatively noisy for waterfowl, especially during the breeding season, when males chase females, uttering calls that sound like a musical *ka-ka-a-wi*. Females stay motionless and cryptic on their nests to avoid predators, and thus people can come within one metre of the nest before birds may take flight. Throughout the winter and during migration, these ducks congregate in large flocks, sometimes of more than 5,000 individuals.

PHOTO: MARK MALLORY

RESEARCH AND MONITORING

Studies of long-tailed duck breeding have been conducted in the Queen Maud Gulf Migratory Bird Sanctuary, and in Queen's Channel in the High Arctic. These ducks are counted as part of general waterfowl surveys, but they are often cryptic and they dive underwater, making it difficult to count them reliably.

SURVIVAL AND STATUS

These ducks are common—probably the most common ducks in Nunavut—but they are poorly surveyed during the breeding season or winter. The population is in decline in the western Arctic, but scientists are not sure of the population status in the eastern Arctic. There are around 800,000 long-tailed ducks in Arctic Canada. Long-tailed ducks are eaten by peregrine falcons and gyrfalcons, and their nests may be depredated by Arctic foxes, as well as glaucous or herring gulls and jaegers.

LOCAL ECOLOGICAL KNOWLEDGE

Inuit used long-tailed ducks to identify the time of year when someone was born. If you were born during the spring or summer, you were an *aggiarjuk* (long-tailed duck). If you were born during the fall or winter, you were an *aqiggiq* (ptarmigan).

PHOTO: TYLER ROSS

DID YOU KNOW?

Long-tailed ducks used to be called "Oldsquaw" in North America, but their common name was changed to be consistent with their name in Europe.

PHOTO: MARK PECK

FAMILY ANATIDAE

Red-breasted Merganser

INUKTITUT NAME
Kajjiqtuuq

FRENCH NAME
Harle huppé

SCIENTIFIC NAME
Mergus serrator

APPEARANCE

Dimorphic. This large diving duck weighs 800 to 1,350 grams, and has a wingspan of 74 centimetres. Breeding males have dark, metallic-green heads with long feathers at the back that split into double-pointed crests. They have white collars around their necks, reddish-brown breasts speckled with black, bold white lines between their black backs and grey sides, white and black checkered patterns on their upper backs, and white underparts. Females have reddish-brown heads with shaggy crests, and brown necks. Grey feathers cover their backs, sides, and tails, while their chins, throats, breasts, and bellies are white. Members of both sexes have a long, narrow, serrated orange bill and orange legs and feet.

Breeding Only

RANGE

This bird is found across mainland Nunavut, southern Baffin Island, and in a few isolated locations in the High Arctic (parts of Victoria Island and west of Pond Inlet). They spend the winter in shallow areas along the Pacific and Atlantic coasts.

HABITAT

In Nunavut, this duck is found breeding near freshwater ponds, pools, and rivers, and occasionally close to the marine coastline or on islands. During the breeding season, they forage in shallow (less than five metres deep) freshwater and saltwater, often at the mouths of rivers. They winter along shallow, calm marine coasts.

DIET

Carnivore. Mergansers mostly eat small fish, but they also consume crustaceans, insects, worms, and amphibians.

REPRODUCTION

Red-breasted mergansers nest in hollows or depressions in rocks or the ground, among taller vegetation if available. The female builds the nest and lines it with vegetation and downy feathers, and then lays five to eleven pale greyish-white eggs. Only the female incubates and rears the young; the male leaves early in incubation to moult his flight feathers. During brood-rearing, different groups of merganser ducklings will merge together to form crèches, accompanied by one or more mothers.

BEHAVIOUR

Red-breasted mergansers are gregarious most of the year, sometimes nesting in loose colonies with Arctic terns and gulls, and often feeding in flocks.

SURVIVAL AND STATUS

Breeding populations of this duck have not been well surveyed, so many counts are from migrating or wintering birds. The Canadian and Alaskan populations are estimated to be about 250,000 birds, but scientists do not know how many of these are in Nunavut (probably a small number). The population is thought to be declining in eastern North America.

DID YOU KNOW?

Adult red-breasted mergansers will dive and work together as a group to drive fish into the shallows where they can catch them, just like dolphins or whales sometimes do.

PHOTO: SHAWN CRAIK

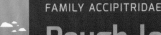

Rough-legged Hawk

INUKTITUT NAME
Qinnuajuaq; kaajuuq

FRENCH NAME
Buse pattue

SCIENTIFIC NAME
Buteo lagopus

PHOTO: ENVIRONMENT CANADA, CHARLES FRANCIS

APPEARANCE

Polymorphic. This is a large raptor that weighs 750 to 1,400 grams (the females being heavier than the males) and has a wingspan up to 140 centimetres. The rough-legged hawk is known for having much variation in its appearance. The adult male light morph has greyish-brown upperparts covered with irregular, light-coloured mottling. On its underside, it is heavily mottled with grey and brown, often appearing to have a pale band across the breast. The underwings are barred with brownish black but appear mostly whitish, and have a distinctive dark patch on the front centre ("wrist"). The female light morph looks like the male, but the belly is often all dark, the breast is more tan coloured, and the upperparts of the female are browner. The male dark morph is blackish brown all over, with some lighter barring on the tail and outer wings. The head is light brown, with a notably light eyebrow and forehead and a darker line through the eye. The female dark morph is more brown everywhere than the male. Adult birds can exhibit a range of dark and light colouration anywhere between these morph extremes. Rough-legged hawks have feathers down their legs to their feet, and have orange-yellow bills, legs, and feet.

RANGE

Breeding

The rough-legged hawk is a bird of the tundra and taiga. It is found across all of Nunavut south of 75°N, although there are records of it nesting on Ellesmere and Devon Islands. It is uncommon on the northern half of Baffin Island. It spends the winter throughout the continental United States, except for the southeast.

HABITAT

This hawk occupies open tundra areas, provided that nesting sites are nearby. Nests are located on cliffs in mountainous areas, along marine coastlines, in rock outcrops, and along river valleys. In the winter, it frequents open areas in the south that mimic tundra habitats.

DIET

Carnivore. The rough-legged hawk consumes lemmings, ground squirrels, and Arctic hare, as well as birds.

PHOTO: DOROTHY TOOTOO

REPRODUCTION

The male partner selects the nest site and gathers most of the nesting materials, and the female constructs the nest. The nests are typically a bulky mass of sticks, lined with vegetation, small twigs, and feathers from prey. The female lays two to seven greenish-blue eggs (sometimes pale tan) blotched with reddish brown, and the female does almost all of the incubation, although the male and female both bring food for the young. Clutches are larger in years with more lemmings.

BEHAVIOUR

Unlike falcons, which take their prey in the air, rough-legged hawks typically perch or hang high in the air, spot their targets, and descend on them vertically to pounce on them on the ground. With suitable wind, they are often seen hovering in the air, with their heads shifting side to side as they scan for prey. These hawks are generally solitary birds, although they may form small flocks and roost together in the winter.

RESEARCH AND MONITORING

Studies of rough-legged hawks have been undertaken near the Kent Peninsula in the Kitikmeot region, as well as near the Perry and Thelon rivers.

SURVIVAL AND STATUS

There are no good estimates of the North American population of this species, but some pooled counts suggest that there are at least 50,000 rough-legged hawks. There is no evidence of any change in their population. Foxes, wolves, bears, and jaegers are potential predators of hawk eggs and young, although success rates of predation on hawk nests are probably low.

DID YOU KNOW?

Although there are many hawk species in North America, the rough-legged hawk is the only one found on the tundra. Along with falcons and snowy owls, it is one of the few large raptors found across most of Nunavut.

FAMILY FALCONIDAE

Gyrfalcon

INUKTITUT NAME
Kiggavik

FRENCH NAME
Faucon gerfaut

SCIENTIFIC NAME
Falco rusticolis

PHOTO: MIKE MCEVOY

APPEARANCE

Monomorphic. This large raptor—the largest of all falcons (the females being 30% larger than the males)—weighs 1.1 to 1.8 kilograms and has a wingspan up to 120 centimetres. This means that there is marked sexual dimorphism in size, but not in the appearance of the feathers. Gyrfalcons occur in three colour variants (not truly morphs). The most stunning is the white variant, where the entire bird is white with brownish-black dots, bars, and streaks, somewhat similar to a snowy owl, although the falcon is more tapered overall. The dark variant is generally dark brownish, with pale grey streaked or barred feathers and brown on the breast and belly. The grey variant is an intermediate between these, but generally with a white to pale brown barred and spotted breast and belly. This variant also has grey and brown barred wings, with a neutral grey upper side spotted, streaked, or barred with darker grey. The forehead, crown, nape, and cheeks are whitish brown, with a distinctive darker grey strip through the eye. The bill, legs, and feet vary from yellow to bluish grey. Gyrfalcons are larger than peregrine falcons, and have conspicuously large tails.

Breeding Only

RANGE

The gyrfalcon breeds across all of Nunavut except for the low, flat islands, which include Prince Charles, Bathurst, Cornwallis, Amund Ringnes, and Ellef Ringnes. In fact, its breeding range is markedly similar to that of rock ptarmigan. In the winter, it forages in open areas across Canada and the northern United States.

HABITAT

This falcon is commonly found near open Arctic and alpine tundra, and along rivers and seacoasts where cliffs and rock outcrops provide nesting sites. At times it may be found out on the sea ice near polynyas. In the winter, it frequents open habitats and hunts near bird concentrations, such as those found near reservoirs.

DIET

Carnivore. The gyrfalcon is a ptarmigan specialist, feeding principally on these birds in the breeding season. However, year-round it also eats other birds, especially waterfowl and seabirds, as well as Arctic hare and lemmings.

REPRODUCTION

Gyrfalcons appear to rarely build their own nests, and instead reuse old nest sites, or take over sites formerly built by common ravens, rough-legged hawks, or golden eagles. The female usually lays one to five white to reddish-brown eggs (colour highly variable). Both parents incubate eggs and help rear the chicks.

PHOTO: PIERRE RICHARD

BEHAVIOUR

Young gyrfalcons remain in their nests for over a month, and when they have to defecate, they back up to the side of the nest and release their feces. This material is white and builds up over the years, and can become several metres deep in certain locations. Like other falcons, gyrfalcons rely on speed to swoop in and catch prey, and they can dive at more than 200 kilometres per hour.

RESEARCH AND MONITORING

Studies have been conducted on gyrfalcons on Ellesmere Island and near the Kent Peninsula in the Kitikmeot region. Researchers have also recorded data on gyrfalcons feeding on seabirds in places such as the Digges Islands.

SURVIVAL AND STATUS

There are an estimated 5,000 gyrfalcons in Nunavut and the Northwest Territories, and their numbers appear to be stable. They have few predators except other falcons and eagles.

DID YOU KNOW?

Gyrfalcons are the prized falcon in many Middle Eastern countries, where royalty use falcons to hunt.

Peregrine Falcon

PHOTO: JIM RICHARDS

INUKTITUT NAME
Kiggaviarjuk

FRENCH NAME
Faucon pèlerin

SCIENTIFIC NAME
Falco peregrinus (subspecies *tundrius, anatum, pealei*)

APPEARANCE

Monomorphic. This is a large raptor that weighs 500 to 1,100 grams and has a wingspan up to 110 centimetres, the females being 20% larger and 50% heavier than the males. There is strong sexual dimorphism in size, but not in feather appearance. Adults have bluish-grey upperparts, nearly black heads, and whitish-grey underparts heavily barred with black. The peregrine falcon's face has a distinctive vertical black facial stripe from the eye down towards the breast resembling a broad moustache, often highlighted by paler feathers on the cheek. Its bill, legs, and feet are yellow, and there is a distinctive yellow ring around the eye. It has long, black talons. Peregrines are smaller and sleeker than gyrfalcons, and have smaller tails.

Breeding Only

RANGE

The peregrine falcon breeds across all of Nunavut to approximately 72°N, and is uncommon or absent from most of the High Arctic islands. *F. p. tundrius* is the principal subspecies here, although *F. p. anatum* may occur in the southern and western portions of Nunavut. Depending on their breeding locations, peregrines migrate through the continent or along the coasts to the Caribbean and South America for the winter.

HABITAT

This falcon shows little to no habitat preference in open country, other than typically having nest sites on cliffs or rock outcrops. They are common near seabird colonies.

DIET

Carnivore. The peregrine falcon has a broad diet consisting of bats and hundreds of species of birds and small rodents. In Nunavut, peregrines consume ptarmigan, shorebirds, longspurs, buntings, larks, and small seabirds, as well as lemmings. Most prey are taken in the air.

REPRODUCTION

Peregrine falcons typically nest in scrapes on cliff ledges, which they sometimes line with vegetation, but they may take over previous nests from another species, like ravens. Usually the male makes several scrapes, and the female chooses one for nesting. The female usually lays three to four creamy-white eggs heavily marked with reddish-brown spots. Both parents incubate the eggs and help rear the chicks.

BEHAVIOUR

Peregrines are amazing in flight and can perform impressive feats, including rolling over so that they are on their backs in mid-air (ravens also do this). During courtship, mates may pass food to each other while flying. Peregrine falcons are the fastest animals in Nunavut, able to dive at their prey at speeds of 320 kilometres per hour.

PHOTO: JIM RICHARDS

RESEARCH AND MONITORING

Peregrine falcon studies have been conducted near Rankin Inlet, as well as incidental observations and research at other locations near seabird colonies, such as Coats Island and Digges Sound.

SURVIVAL AND STATUS

There are an estimated 50,000 peregrine falcons in North America, of which perhaps 12,000 are from Arctic Canada. All subspecies of peregrines are identified as being at least of special concern by COSEWIC, although populations have exhibited a strong recovery after numbers in the twentieth century dwindled due to persecution and contaminants in their food webs. By 2000, their numbers were still increasing. Peregrines have few predators except other falcons and eagles.

DID YOU KNOW?

Peregrines are one of the most broadly distributed terrestrial vertebrates, found in deserts, in wetlands, on islands, in forests, and from the tundra to the tropics and the mountains to the plains. They are found on every continent except Antarctica.

FAMILY GRUIDAE

Sandhill Crane

INUKTITUT NAME
Tatiggaq; tatiggarjuaq

FRENCH NAME
Grue de Canada

SCIENTIFIC NAME
Grus canadensis

PHOTO: LISA PIRIE

APPEARANCE

Monomorphic. This is a very large, long-necked, long-legged bird that weighs 3 to 4.5 kilograms and has a wingspan of up to 230 centimetres. It is the tallest bird in Nunavut, standing up to 120 centimetres high. Sandhill cranes are unmistakable, with grey feathers over their entire bodies except for red foreheads and crowns, and white patches from cheek to chin. Their bills and legs are black. Sometimes their feathers may be stained rusty brown.

Breeding Only

RANGE

This crane is found in the Low and High Arctic, but is more common south of 74°N. They may nest in any appropriate habitat in this range, except for the southern half of Baffin Island. These birds migrate over much of North America to spend the winter in the southern United States and northern Mexico.

HABITAT

Sandhill cranes nest in low, wet marsh or sedge meadows near tundra ponds, and they feed in similar habitats. During migration they frequent large marshes and agricultural fields, and they winter in these habitats as well as in coastal wetlands.

DIET

Omnivore. This bird eats insects, mollusks, small birds, and mammals, as well as seeds, berries, and the thick parts of some plant roots. South of Nunavut they also eat reptiles and amphibians.

REPRODUCTION

Sandhill cranes build nests from surrounding vegetation, creating mounds with central depressions. The female lays one to two pale brown to light green eggs speckled with light brown. Both the

male and the female incubate the eggs and rear
the young.

BEHAVIOUR

Sandhill cranes are best known for their
distinctive and elaborate courtship dances, which
see these huge birds spreading their wings and
jumping in the air. They also have bugle-like
calls that can be heard long before the birds are
seen. Sandhill cranes mate for life, and may live
for more than 20 years.

RESEARCH AND MONITORING

Sandhill cranes are counted as part of the
regional shorebird and waterfowl surveys that
occur annually in different parts of Nunavut.

SURVIVAL AND STATUS

There are approximately 700,000 sandhill cranes
in North America, but it is unknown how many
breed in Nunavut. The population is stable and
increasing in some areas. Foxes, ravens, eagles,
and owls are all predators of crane nests.

PHOTO: JIM RICHARDS

DID YOU KNOW?

These cranes will defend their nests against avian and mammalian predators,
spreading their wings to look huge, thrusting their large bills forward, and
eventually jumping up and kicking with their large feet, exposing the predators to
their claws.

FAMILY CHARADRIIDAE
American Golden Plover

INUKTITUT NAME
Tuulliq; tuulligaarjuk; ungalitte

FRENCH NAME
Pluvier bronzé

SCIENTIFIC NAME
Pluvialis dominica

PHOTO: JIM RICHARDS

APPEARANCE

Dimorphic. This is a large, slender shorebird, weighing 125 to 190 grams and having a wingspan up to 70 centimetres. During the breeding season, males are dark greyish brown from the top of the head through the tail, interspersed with yellow and tan speckles, and have white feathers on the forehead, breast, and sides of the head and neck. They have black faces, necks, and underparts. The females are similar, but are often less well defined in their feather features and are duller and more brownish overall. In both sexes, the bill, legs, and feet are greyish black.

Breeding

RANGE

This plover is found in the Low and High Arctic, but is more common north of 66°N. They nest on the High Arctic Islands except for Ellesmere Island, as well as western Baffin Island, Southampton Island, and the northern mainland. These birds migrate over the Atlantic Ocean to South America for the winter.

HABITAT

American golden plovers nest in dry areas and forage in well-drained, sparsely vegetated tundra. They are not very common along coastlines except during migration. They tend to move their young to moister habitats for chick rearing. In the winter, they are most common on grasslands and agricultural areas in South America.

DIET

Omnivore. This plover eats terrestrial insects, spiders, and berries on breeding grounds, and adds mollusks, crustaceans, and other plants to its diet during migration and winter.

REPRODUCTION

American golden plovers breed in low densities across the tundra. The male creates several nest scrapes within his territory during courtship with the female, but the female chooses only one scrape and lines it with lichens. She then lays four creamy, tan-coloured eggs heavily marked with brown and black splotches. Both the male and the female incubate the eggs and rear the young.

BEHAVIOUR

Unlike many other shorebirds, these birds often defend small feeding territories during migration and winter. They are highly territorial during breeding, so it is not common to see them in dense aggregations. They exhibit a complex array of distraction behaviours to lure or scare predators away from their nests, including dragging their wings, puffing up, and calling loudly.

RESEARCH AND MONITORING

American golden plovers are counted as part of the regional shorebird surveys that occur intermittently in different parts of Nunavut.

SURVIVAL AND STATUS

There are about 200,000 American golden plovers in North America, a large proportion of which are in Nunavut, although their population is declining. Foxes, falcons, gulls, ravens, and jaegers are all predators of plovers.

DID YOU KNOW?

This plover is one of few birds that are typically darker on their undersides than their topsides during the breeding season.

PHOTO: JIM RICHARDS

Black-bellied Plover

INUKTITUT NAME
Tuuligaarjuk

FRENCH NAME
Pluvier argenté

SCIENTIFIC NAME
Pluvialis squatarola

PHOTO: JIM RICHARDS

APPEARANCE

Dimorphic. This large, bulky shorebird weighs 160 to 250 grams and has a wingspan of up to 80 centimetres. During the breeding season, males have white upperparts, which are mottled and barred with black and a hint of brownish gold. They have solid black underparts from the bill and eye through the chin, throat, breast, and belly. Females have a similar overall pattern, but their upperparts are more subdued, with light and dark brown colouration, and the black on their undersides is often mixed with white. In flight, this plover has black underwing patches where its "armpits" would be, distinguishing it from other plovers. In both sexes, the bill is short and thick, ending in a blunt tip. The bill, legs, and feet are greyish black.

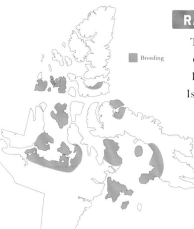

Breeding

RANGE

This plover is found principally in the High Arctic, north of 66°N. It nests on the High Arctic Islands (except for Ellesmere Island), western Baffin Island, Southampton Island, Coats Island, and the northern mainland. This bird winters along the coasts of North America and the Caribbean islands, as well as the coasts of South America.

HABITAT

Black-bellied plovers breed in relatively dry and open lowland tundra with heath vegetation, often near marine coastlines. They often nest on gravelly spots on ridges or slopes. In the winter, they are most common on coastal beaches with sandy to muddy substrates.

DIET

Carnivore. This plover eats terrestrial insects, spiders, mollusks, and small crustaceans throughout the year. In some locations, they may eat seeds and berries in late summer.

REPRODUCTION

The male creates a nest scrape within his territory, which the female may enlarge and line with lichen. The female lays four pinkish, greenish, or brownish eggs with circular dark brown spots on them. Both the male and the female incubate the eggs and rear the young.

BEHAVIOUR

Male black-bellied plovers are fiercely territorial towards all other plovers during the breeding season, and also establish small territories for winter feeding. They tend to forage singly and are rarely in flocks of more than twenty birds when feeding, although they may roost in large flocks. These plovers will kleptoparasitize prey from other shorebirds, and will mob potential predators, like jaegers, with nearby nesting plovers.

RESEARCH AND MONITORING

Black-bellied plovers have been studied at Truelove Lowland on Devon Island, and are counted as part of the regional shorebird surveys that occur intermittently in different parts of Nunavut.

PHOTO: JIM RICHARDS

SURVIVAL AND STATUS

There are about 200,000 of this plover in North America, a large proportion of which are in Nunavut, though their population is declining. Foxes, falcons, gulls, ravens, and jaegers are all predators of plovers.

DID YOU KNOW?

These plovers are one of the few birds that are typically darker on their undersides than their topsides during the breeding season.

FAMILY CHARADRIIDAE

Semipalmated Plover

INUKTITUT NAME
Qulliquliarjuk

FRENCH NAME
Pluvier semipalmé

SCIENTIFIC NAME
Charadrius semipalmatus

PHOTO: CREDENCE WOOD

APPEARANCE

Dimorphic. This small shorebird weighs 45 to 70 grams and has a wingspan of 50 centimetres. The females are larger than the males. During the breeding season, males have a brownish top of the head and back, with a distinctive black mask through the eye that splits to the top of the forehead and to the bill. Males also have black bands around their lower necks and chests, white patches above their bills, and black collars. Their underparts are bright white. Their bills are orange with black tips, and their legs are orange. The female is similar to the male, but duller, with a brownish tinge to the black feathers.

RANGE

The semipalmated plover is widely distributed from the Subarctic to the High Arctic, occurring throughout Nunavut south of 70°N, but excluding most of northern Baffin Island. Plovers spend the winter along the east and west coasts of the United States and Mexico, as well as the Caribbean islands and northern South America.

Breeding

HABITAT

This plover is most common near moist areas. It nests in well-drained, sandy, gravelly, or rocky areas, and forages along the moist edges of lakes, rivers, ponds, or tidal mudflats. During migration and winter, it is common along mudflats and calm beaches.

DIET

Carnivore. Plovers consume terrestrial and aquatic insects, spiders, marine worms, crustaceans, and mollusks.

REPRODUCTION

As with many shorebirds, males arrive and establish a breeding territory and build several scrapes as potential nests. Females arrive a bit later and choose one scrape, laying into it four light brown eggs covered with dark brown or black splotches. Both parents participate in incubation and chick rearing.

PHOTO: CREDENCE WOOD

BEHAVIOUR

Semipalmated plovers are gregarious during migration and in the winter, but their flock sizes are usually small. They are territorial when breeding and usually forage alone. They exhibit classic plover feeding behaviour, whereby they run, pause, pluck prey from the ground, and repeat. These plovers also perform various distraction displays when predators are near their nests or chicks.

RESEARCH AND MONITORING

Semipalmated plovers are counted as part of the regional shorebird surveys that occur intermittently in different parts of Nunavut. There has been some research on their breeding biology on Southampton and Coats Islands.

SURVIVAL AND STATUS

Estimates of the population size of semipalmated plovers are poor, and range from 30,000 to 150,000 birds. Counts in some areas suggest that they are one of the few shorebirds breeding in Nunavut whose population may be increasing. Foxes, falcons, gulls, ravens, and jaegers are all predators of plovers.

PHOTO: JIM RICHARDS

DID YOU KNOW?

Semipalmated plovers locate prey by sight, but may also quiver their feet in the water to make prey move so they can snatch them.

Ruddy Turnstone

INUKTITUT NAME
Taliffak

FRENCH NAME
Tournepierre à collier

SCIENTIFIC NAME
Arenaria interpres

PHOTO: JIM RICHARDS

APPEARANCE

Dimorphic. This medium-sized, stocky shorebird weighs 85 to 190 grams and has a wingspan of 55 centimetres. During the breeding season, males have white heads, black throats, necks, and breasts, and black streaks extending up to their eyes and the backs of their necks. They have bright white underparts. The feathers on their wings and tails are a mottled reddish-chestnut mixed with black and brown patches. The male's legs are orange and their bills are black, chisel shaped, and slightly upturned. In flight, these birds have obvious white backs, rumps, and upper tails. Overall, the female has a similar pattern to the male, except that her crown is more mottled, her breast is more flecked, and generally her colouration is less bright.

RANGE

■ Breeding

Turnstones are found in the Low and High Arctic, most commonly on the High Arctic islands, Southampton Island, the Melville and Boothia peninsulas, and southwestern Baffin Island. The birds winter over a vast coastal area of eastern and western North America, the Caribbean, northern South America, Europe, and northern Africa.

HABITAT

Turnstones breed in tundra along rocky coasts, in drained hummock areas, and near marshes, streams, and ponds. They feed on vegetated tundra during the breeding season, as well as rocky, muddy, or sandy shores of freshwater and saltwater bodies. They are tied to marine coastlines during migration and in the winter.

DIET

Omnivore. Turnstones eat terrestrial insects, spiders, and vegetation during the breeding season, while during migration and in the winter they consume insects, mollusks, crustaceans, worms, eggs of other birds, human garbage, and carrion.

REPRODUCTION

Ruddy turnstones are territorial when breeding and thus they nest at fairly low densities, up to a maximum of four pairs per square kilometre. Although the male makes several nest scrapes during courtship, the female makes the scrape that she will nest in, lines it with lichen strands, and lays three or four greyish-green eggs with irregular brown speckling. Both sexes incubate the eggs, although the female does proportionally more than the male, and both parents rear the chicks.

PHOTO: MARK MALLORY

BEHAVIOUR

These birds are highly gregarious during the winter and migration, occurring in flocks of tens to thousands of birds, but become very territorial during the breeding season. Although turnstones sometimes give distraction displays like other shorebirds, more often they are aggressive and try to drive off predators, even large gulls.

PHOTO: JIM RICHARDS

RESEARCH AND MONITORING

Ruddy turnstones are counted as part of the regional shorebird surveys that occur intermittently in different parts of Nunavut, and there has been some specific research on their breeding biology on Ellesmere and Southampton Islands.

SURVIVAL AND STATUS

There are about 245,000 ruddy turnstones in North America, mostly in Nunavut, though their population is declining. Foxes, falcons, gulls, ravens, and jaegers are all predators of turnstones.

DID YOU KNOW?
Turnstones are so named because of their curious feeding habit of using their bills to flip over small stones in search of aquatic invertebrates.

FAMILY SCOLOPACIDAE
Red Knot

INUKTITUT NAME
Qajorlak; aupaqtuq sigjariarjuk

FRENCH NAME
Bécasseau maubèche

SCIENTIFIC NAME
Colidris canutus
(subspecies *islandica, rufa*)

APPEARANCE

Monomorphic, although males may be brighter. The red knot is a large shorebird that weighs 125 to 205 grams and has a wingspan of 60 centimetres. During the breeding season, the feathers on its eyepatch, lower cheek, breast, and belly are a distinctive salmon to brick-red colour, while its undertail is white. Its back appears spotted black, chestnut, white, and grey and its wings are grey with dark brown primary feathers. The bill and legs are black.

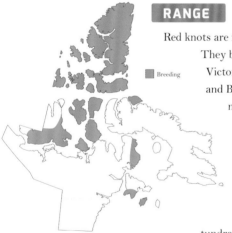

■ Breeding

RANGE

Red knots are found principally in the High Arctic, north of 66°N. They breed on Ellesmere, Devon, Somerset, Prince of Wales, Victoria, and Southampton Islands, as well as on the Melville and Boothia peninsulas. In the winter they fly either to northern Europe, the Caribbean, or South America.

HABITAT

Knots nest near the marine coast on peninsulas or islands, typically on dry, sunny tundra ridges with some vegetation, and sometimes at sites up to 300 metres above sea level. They forage on vegetated tundra during the breeding season, but switch to feeding in intertidal coastlines in water less than three centimetres deep during migration and winter.

DIET

Omnivore. Knots eat terrestrial insects and vegetation when they are on their breeding grounds, but their diet shifts to small mollusks, crustaceans, and worms during migration and winter. In particular, they specialize in feeding on the eggs of horseshoe crabs.

REPRODUCTION

Knot nests are dispersed across the tundra, even in preferred habitats, with nests lying generally more than one kilometre apart. The male arrives first on the territory and prepares three to five nest scrapes, from which the female will choose one to use. She then lays four olive-green eggs covered with dark brown blotches. Both the male and the female take turns incubating the eggs, but the male rears the brood.

PHOTO: JENNIE RAUSCH

BEHAVIOUR

Knots are gregarious during winter, migration, and feeding. People have observed knots feeding as densely as 20 per square metre in areas rich with food. Huge flocks of tens of thousands of birds may occur on key beaches during migration, making them highly sensitive to disturbance. Like other shorebirds, knots perform distraction displays if scared off their nests, particularly if their eggs are almost hatched.

RESEARCH AND MONITORING

Red knots are counted in regional shorebird surveys in different parts of Nunavut. Research on their migrations and breeding biology has been conducted on northern Ellesmere Island, and migration tracking has also been undertaken on Southampton Island.

SURVIVAL AND STATUS

The combined total population of all races of red knots is approximately 1 million birds, but their population is declining. In particular, the *C. c. rufa* race is considered by COSEWIC to be endangered in Canada, and the *C. c. islandica* race is considered to be of special concern. Foxes, falcons, gulls, ravens, and jaegers are all predators of knots.

DID YOU KNOW?

Certain populations of red knots migrate from Nunavut all the way to southern South America, a distance of approximately 15,000 kilometres one way!

FAMILY SCOLOPACIDAE

Sanderling

INUKTITUT NAME
Sigjariarjuk

FRENCH NAME
Bécasseau sanderling

SCIENTIFIC NAME
Calidris alba

APPEARANCE

Monomorphic. This medium-sized, plump shorebird weighs 40 to 100 grams and has a wingspan of 45 centimetres. Adults are reddish above and white below during the Arctic breeding season. Their heads, breasts, backs, wings, and tails are reddish to sandy brown and coarsely mottled with dark and pale black and tans, which creates a clear contrast to their white chests and underparts. Their bills are short, stout, and black, and their legs are short and black.

Breeding Only

RANGE

Sanderlings breed mostly in the High Arctic above 66°N, except for parts of Southampton Island and the Melville Peninsula. In the winter, they may be found almost anywhere along the coasts of North and South America.

HABITAT

This shorebird will nest in a range of habitats, but most nests are on gravelly, well-drained ridge tops; gentle, dry slopes; flat, drained sedge meadows; or barren tundra plains. They feed in damp tundra or along the edges of streams, ponds, lakes, and sandy beaches. In the winter, they are principally associated with sandy beaches, although they can also be found on mudflats, lagoons, and intertidal rocky shorelines.

DIET

Carnivore. These sandpipers eat terrestrial insects, spiders, worms, mollusks, and crustaceans.

REPRODUCTION

Sanderlings are territorial during breeding; they disperse their nests across the tundra at low densities, with a maximum of three pairs per square kilometre. The female makes a nest scrape in the breeding territory, lines it with leaves and lichens, and then lays four olive-green to brownish to bluish-green eggs with many dark brown spots (eggs quite variable). Both sexes incubate the eggs and rear the chicks. Sometimes sanderling females lay a second set of eggs. In these cases, the male incubates and rears young from the first nest and the female does so for young from the second.

PHOTO: LINDSAY ARMER

BEHAVIOUR

These birds are gregarious during migration and in the winter, usually in small flocks of 5 to 30 birds, although some individuals defend small feeding areas. This species is often observed in mixed flocks with other species of shorebirds. Sanderlings are noted for being excellent runners, and characteristically rush out from shore as waves recede to check the sand for stranded prey, running back up the beach before the next wave.

PHOTO: MIKE MCEVOY

RESEARCH AND MONITORING

Sanderlings are counted as part of the regional shorebird surveys that occur intermittently in different parts of Nunavut.

SURVIVAL AND STATUS

Sanderlings are common in some regions of Nunavut, and mostly occur where there are few people. There are more than 300,000 sanderlings in Arctic Canada, mostly from Nunavut, but their populations are declining rapidly, due in part to disturbance and loss of sandy beach habitats in their wintering grounds. Like most other shorebirds, foxes, falcons, gulls, ravens, and jaegers are all predators of sanderlings.

DID YOU KNOW?

The sanderling may be the best-known shorebird in the world. It is broadly distributed along the coasts of North and South America in the winter, from 50°N to 50°S, particularly along beaches where people are likely to be.

Purple Sandpiper

INUKTITUT NAME
Segalea; Tudlik; saarfaarsuk

FRENCH NAME
Bécasseau violet

SCIENTIFIC NAME
Calidris maritima

PHOTO: MARK ELDERKIN

APPEARANCE

Monomorphic. This is a medium-sized, chubby shorebird, the females being a bit larger than males. They weigh 50 to 100 grams and have wingspans of up to 45 centimetres. Adults appear dark with brightly fringed feathers during the Arctic breeding season. Their necks and backs have blackish-brown feathers with strong, light, tan-coloured fringing that gives the bird a mottled appearance. Their rump and central tail feathers are black, and their breasts and undersides are white with dark spotting. The bases of their bills and their legs are a dull olive brown. Why are they called "purple"? Their winter plumage is a dark, slate-coloured purple!

Breeding Only

RANGE

Purple sandpipers breed principally in the eastern Canadian Arctic—Baffin Island and the High Arctic Islands—as well as Southampton and Coats islands. They are one of the most northerly wintering shorebirds, staying along the eastern coast of the United States and Canada.

HABITAT

This shorebird has a range of suitable nesting habitats, including mossy or lichen tundra, gravel ridges, and rocky beaches. They can be found nesting inland up to 300 metres above sea level. They feed in moss or lichen uplands, along the edges of pools or beaches, and in the intertidal zone. They are one of the most common wintering shorebirds along rocky coastlines of eastern North America and Greenland.

DIET

Omnivore. These sandpipers eat terrestrial insects, spiders, snails, worms, mollusks, and crustaceans, as well as seeds and berries.

REPRODUCTION

Purple sandpipers nest in low densities across the tundra, with less than one nest per square kilometre. The male makes several scrapes in the ground in his territory, and the female chooses one, lines it with vegetation, and lays three to four pale, greenish-beige eggs with many dark brown blotches. The male undertakes most of the incubation and chick rearing.

PHOTO: MARK MALLORY

BEHAVIOUR

These birds are not as gregarious as other sandpipers, generally being seen in smaller flocks of a few to tens of birds. However, they are quite tame and approachable.

RESEARCH AND MONITORING

Purple sandpipers are counted as part of the regional shorebird surveys that occur intermittently in different parts of Nunavut.

SURVIVAL AND STATUS

Purple sandpipers are locally common in some regions of Nunavut, but at low densities. There are an estimated 25,000 of these birds in Canada, and their numbers are thought to be declining. Like most other shorebirds, foxes, falcons, gulls, ravens, and jaegers are all predators of sandpipers.

DID YOU KNOW?

The distraction display of the purple sandpiper is an interesting sight! This species raises its feathers to look like fur and drags its wings on the ground to look like it has four legs. It then emits loud squeaks and scurries about, resembling a lemming on the tundra. A predator often falls for this act, and is drawn away from the bird's nest or young.

PHOTO: MARK ELDERKIN

FAMILY SCOLOPACIDAE

Semipalmated Sandpiper

INUKTITUT NAME
Higyariak

FRENCH NAME
Béccasseau semipalmé

SCIENTIFIC NAME
Calidris pusilla

APPEARANCE

Monomorphic. In many ways, the semipalmated sandpiper is the quintessential, nondescript "little brown bird" found in many coastal areas. This is a very small shorebird, 20 to 35 grams with a 35-centimetre wingspan. The females are slightly larger than the males. In the Arctic breeding season, sandpipers are brown above and white below, with tan and brown streaking their throats and chests. They have streaked, greyish-brown heads, backs, and wings. They have dark brown blotches on their backs, with paler brown or tan speckling on the sides of their heads and necks, and a line made from darker brown feathers through their eyes. Their lower chests, bellies, and underparts are white, while their legs and bills are black.

RANGE

Semipalmated sandpipers breed in the Low and High Arctic, generally south of 70°N. This includes the Nunavut mainland, Southampton and Victoria Islands, the islands in Foxe Basin, southwestern Baffin Island, and the Melville and Boothia Peninsulas. These birds spend the winter along the coastlines of Central and South America.

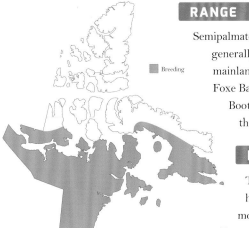

Breeding

HABITAT

This shorebird has a range of suitable nesting habitats, but is primarily found in drained areas with moist tundra and in sandy habitats. It forages in marine mudflats and very shallow edges of freshwater ponds and lakes year-round.

DIET

Carnivore. These sandpipers eat marine crustaceans, mollusks, and worms, as well as terrestrial insects and spiders.

REPRODUCTION

Semipalmated sandpipers are territorial and not social during the breeding season. Males establish a territory (often the one used the previous year) and make several nest scrapes, from which the female will choose one in which to lay her three to four olive to tan eggs, which have irregular, liver-coloured splotching (egg colour is quite variable for this species). Both the male and female take turns incubating the nest and rearing the chicks, although the female abandons the chicks first.

BEHAVIOUR

These birds are extremely gregarious during migration and in the winter, with up to 300,000 birds flocking together on a single beach, but they are not social during breeding. When a predator is near their nests, they typically stay motionless to avoid detection, but, if spotted, they perform distraction displays to coerce predators away from their nests, including a display that mimics a rodent running across the tundra.

PHOTO: JIM RICHARDS

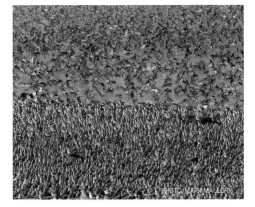

PHOTO: MARK MALLORY

RESEARCH AND MONITORING

Semipalmated sandpipers are counted as part of the regional shorebird surveys that occur intermittently in different parts of Nunavut.

SURVIVAL AND STATUS

Semipalmated sandpipers are one of the most abundant species of shorebirds in North America, with a population estimated at 2 to 3.5 million birds; however, this population is thought to be declining. As they are with most other shorebirds, foxes, falcons, gulls, ravens, and jaegers are all predators of sandpipers. Peregrine falcons may be particularly important predators at migration stopovers.

DID YOU KNOW?

This sandpiper is referred to as one of the "peeps" by bird watchers, because it is tiny and emits a peeping call. Many bird watchers stop to see the enormous flocks of these birds in the Bay of Fundy in New Brunswick, before the birds depart on a non-stop, 4,000-kilometre flight to South America.

White-rumped Sandpiper

INUKTITUT NAME
Sijjariarjuk

FRENCH NAME
Béccasseau à croupion blanc

SCIENTIFIC NAME
Calidris fuscicollis

PHOTO: MIKE MCEVOY

APPEARANCE

Monomorphic. The white-rumped sandpiper is a small shorebird—40 to 60 grams with a 45-centimetre wingspan—and is highly streaked with brown above and white below. In the Arctic breeding season, they have streaked, greyish-brown heads, backs, and wings, with dark brown blotches on their backs, paler brown or tan speckling on the sides of their heads and necks, and lines made from darker brown feathers through their eyes. Their breasts are pale grey with dark brown streaks. The feathers on their crowns tend to be pinkish brown with dark streaks. Their lower chests, bellies, and underparts are white, and they have distinctive white patches at the bases of their tails. Their legs and bills are black.

■ Breeding

RANGE

White-rumped sandpipers breed in the Low and High Arctic, generally between 66°N and 76°N. They can be found on all of the islands south of Ellesmere Island and north of Southampton Island, as well as the coastal Nunavut mainland, including the Melville Peninsula. They spend the winter along the coastlines of southern South America.

HABITAT

This shorebird is found in moist, well-vegetated tundra and wet meadows in low-lying areas, generally around marshy ponds, lakes, or streams, and feeds in these habitats. During migration and in the winter, it frequents both freshwater and salt marshes, but is uncommon on sandy beaches.

DIET

Omnivore. These sandpipers eat insects, small mollusks, and worms, as well as some seeds.

REPRODUCTION

White-rumped sandpipers are territorial and not social during the breeding season. The male establishes a territory in which the female chooses and scrapes a nest site, usually on a small mound in a moist area. She lays four olive-tan eggs with irregular, reddish-brown splotching. Only the female incubates eggs and rears the chicks.

BEHAVIOUR

These birds are gregarious during migration and in the winter, and although territorial near their nests, they may feed in small groups during the breeding season. They are often observed mixed with other sandpipers. Like other sandpipers, female white-rumped sandpipers perform distraction displays by pretending to be injured if a predator spots them near their nest.

RESEARCH AND MONITORING

White-rumped sandpipers are counted as part of regional shorebird surveys that occur intermittently in different parts of Nunavut.

SURVIVAL AND STATUS

White-rumped sandpipers are abundant in North America, with a population estimated at 1.1 million birds, many of which breed in Nunavut. The number of white-rumped sandpipers is thought to be stable. As they are with most other shorebirds, foxes, falcons, gulls, ravens, and jaegers are all predators of white-rumped sandpipers.

DID YOU KNOW?

Prince Charles Island, a large, low, wet island in Foxe Basin, may support the world's highest concentration and number of white-rumped sandpipers. White-rumped sandpipers also make one of the longest migrations of North American shorebirds—approximately 20,000 kilometres one way!

Baird's Sandpiper

INUKTITUT NAME
Tuvvititiqkiuq

FRENCH NAME
Béccasseau de Baird

SCIENTIFIC NAME
Calidris bairdii

PHOTO: JIM RICHARDS

APPEARANCE

Monomorphic. This is a small shorebird, weighing 30 to 55 grams and having a 47-centimetre wingspan. In the Arctic breeding season, their crowns, napes, mantles (shoulders), and the feathers covering their wings appear like large scales, with dark brown centres and light silver-brown edges, ultimately making their backs appear somewhat silvery with black spots. Their rumps and tails are blackish brown. They have a lighter brown stripe above the eye and a dark brown stripe through the eye, with a dark patch between the eye and bill. Their chins and throats are white, but their upper breasts are streaked with pale brown. Their chests, bellies, and undertails are bright white. Their legs and bills are short and black.

Breeding

RANGE

Baird's sandpiper is a High Arctic species, found north of 66°N. This includes the northern edge of the Nunavut mainland, the northern half of Baffin Island, and the High Arctic Islands. They spend the winter along the coastlines of South America.

HABITAT

This shorebird prefers dry, well-drained, exposed tundra containing minimal vegetation, which may be lichen or heather. It forages in dry areas with short vegetation in the winter.

DIET

Carnivore. These sandpipers eat insects, spiders, and small crustaceans.

REPRODUCTION

Baird's sandpipers are territorial, with territories defended by the males. Both parents build the nest scrape and line it with a few lichens or leaves. The female lays four pale grey eggs, which are darkly splotched with brown and lavender. Both the male and the female take turns incubating the nest and rearing the chicks.

BEHAVIOUR

These birds are territorial during breeding but gregarious during migration and in the winter, usually occurring in small flocks of generally less than 100 birds (although thousands may occur together sometimes in the wintering grounds). Baird's sandpipers exhibit an array of distraction displays to lure predators from their nests.

RESEARCH AND MONITORING

Baird's sandpipers have been studied on Bylot and Victoria Islands and the Melville Peninsula, and are counted as part of regional shorebird surveys that occur intermittently in different parts of Nunavut.

SURVIVAL AND STATUS

There are an estimated 300,000 of these birds in North America, and population trends are unclear but probably declining. They seem to be stable in some locations, such as the Rasmussen Lowlands near Taloyoak. As they are with most other shorebirds, foxes, falcons, gulls, ravens, and jaegers are all predators of sandpipers.

DID YOU KNOW?

This sandpiper makes a huge investment in its eggs. The four eggs represent 120% of the female's body mass, and are produced in just four days!

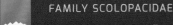

FAMILY SCOLOPACIDAE

Pectoral Sandpiper

INUKTITUT NAME
Sigjariarjuk

FRENCH NAME
Béccasseau à poitrine cendrée

SCIENTIFIC NAME
Calidris melanotos

PHOTO: JIM RICHARDS

APPEARANCE

Monomorphic. This is a medium-sized shorebird, weighing 50 to 125 grams (the males being larger than the females) and having a 49-centimetre wingspan. In the Arctic breeding season, the pectoral sandpiper's crown, nape, mantle (shoulders), and wings appear largely mottled (streaked on the crown), with dark, blackish-brown feather centres fringed with light brown. The side of its head is streaked with light and dark brown, which leaves a lighter brown stripe above the eye. Its rump and tail are blackish brown, and in flight its outer feathers are dark brown. Its chin and throat are white but its breast is heavily streaked with light and dark brown, and ends in an abrupt, distinctive break from the white belly. Its belly and undertail are bright white, while its legs are distinctively yellowish or greenish. Its short bill is dark greenish with an orange base, and slightly downcurved.

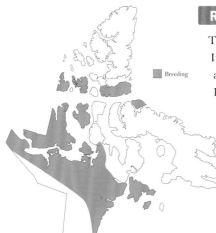

Breeding

RANGE

The pectoral sandpiper is found in the Low and High Arctic. It breeds across the northern coastal plains of the Kivalliq and Kitikmeot regions, as well as Southampton, Devon, Bathurst, Prince of Wales, Victoria, King William, and northern Bylot islands. It spends the winter in central and southern South America.

HABITAT

This shorebird prefers flat, marshy, coastal tundra with some raised ridges and hummocks on which to nest. It forages in wet, grassy areas in the winter.

DIET

Carnivore. These sandpipers eat insects and spiders, but will also feed on small crustaceans. During migration they occasionally consume algae or seeds.

REPRODUCTION

Male pectoral sandpipers are territorial. The female alone chooses the nest site and builds the scrape, lining it with dead grasses, lichen, mosses, and willow. The female lays four pale white eggs, which are darkly splotched with brown and lavender, and she alone incubates and rears the brood.

BEHAVIOUR

This sandpiper is relatively solitary, observed singly or in small groups at most times of the year. Pectoral sandpipers are polygynous or promiscuous, meaning that one male mates with more than one female during the breeding season. Rather than distraction displays, this species tends to crouch low and remain motionless when predators are nearby.

PHOTO: JIM RICHARDS

RESEARCH AND MONITORING

Pectoral sandpipers have been studied on Victoria Island and the Boothia Peninsula, and are counted as part of the regional shorebird surveys that occur intermittently in different parts of Nunavut.

SURVIVAL AND STATUS

There are an estimated 500,000 of these birds in North America, but its population trend is unclear, making it one of the few shorebirds that is not in obvious population decline. Foxes, falcons, gulls, ravens, and jaegers are all predators of sandpipers.

DID YOU KNOW?

This sandpiper has an inflatable throat sac, used to make distinctive hooting noises during courtship.

FAMILY SCOLOPACIDAE

Stilt Sandpiper

INUKTITUT NAME
Sijjariaq; sigjariaq

FRENCH NAME
Béccasseau à échasses

SCIENTIFIC NAME
Calidris himantopus

PHOTO: JIM RICHARDS

APPEARANCE

Monomorphic. This is a medium-sized, slender shorebird, weighing 50 to 80 grams (the females being slightly larger than the males) and having a 47-centimetre wingspan. In the Arctic breeding season, their upperparts are brownish black and their feathers have black centres with whitish edges, giving these sandpipers a striking, dark, streaked appearance. Their outer wing feathers are brown. They have distinct, reddish-brown (chestnut) feathers between their eyes and bills and on their upper cheeks, as well as chestnut streaks on their crowns and napes. The rest of their faces and necks are whitish but streaked with brown. Their chins through to their bellies are a light, brownish-white colour that may be heavily streaked with dark brownish grey. Their chests, flanks, bellies, and undertails often show horizontal barring with dark brownish grey, although the barring is blacker in males. Their bills are straight and dark greenish, and their legs are long and greenish yellow. When flying, their legs extend beyond their tails.

Breeding

RANGE

The stilt sandpiper has a relatively small breeding range in Nunavut, being found principally along southern Victoria Island, Jenny Lind Island, and the Boothia Peninsula. They spend the winter in central South America, although some may remain in Mexico rather than travelling farther south.

HABITAT

This shorebird's habitat preferences are variable, from wet, moist tundra to drier slopes, but in all cases it prefers vegetated locations. It forages in marshes, pools, and pond margins year-round.

DIET

Omnivore. These sandpipers eat both terrestrial and aquatic insects, as well as seeds. They feed principally in water that is belly deep, often submerging their heads to capture prey, a distinctive technique among shorebirds in Nunavut.

REPRODUCTION

Stilt sandpipers are territorial during the breeding season. The male makes several scrapes in a territory, of which the female selects one, then adjusts it to her body and lines it with vegetation. Old nest sites are often reused. The female lays four light to olive-green eggs covered in extensive brown speckling and blotching. Both the male and the female take turns incubating and rearing the chicks.

PHOTO: JIM RICHARDS

BEHAVIOUR

This sandpiper is relatively solitary, observed singly or in small groups at most times of the year, although it can form dense, multi-species flocks during migration. It tends to sit tight on its nest in the presence of a predator, but will also produce distraction displays.

RESEARCH AND MONITORING

Stilt sandpipers have been studied on Victoria Island, and are counted in the regional shorebird surveys that occur intermittently in different parts of Nunavut.

SURVIVAL AND STATUS

There are an estimated 820,000 of these birds in North America, and their population trend is unclear but possibly stable. Foxes, falcons, gulls, ravens, and jaegers are all predators of sandpipers.

DID YOU KNOW?

Because of its large size, this sandpiper was often shot mistakenly with other larger shorebirds when flocks were heavily hunted in the 1800s and early 1900s, leading to a major decline in its population.

Buff-breasted Sandpiper

INUKTITUT NAME
Sijjariaq

FRENCH NAME
Béccasseau roussârte

SCIENTIFIC NAME
Tryngites subruficollis

PHOTO: ENVIRONMENT CANADA, CHARLES FRANCIS

APPEARANCE

Monomorphic. This medium-sized, slender, elegant shorebird weighs 46 to 78 grams and has a 47-centimetre wingspan. The males are larger than the females. During the Arctic breeding season, the feathers on their upperparts (backs, wing covers, upper tails) are deep chocolate brown with pale, soft brown (buff) fringes, somewhat resembling scales. Their heads and underparts are buffish brown, with darker brown streaks on the crown, nape, and sides of their breasts. Their chin and throat areas may be whitish. Their bellies and undertails are whitish. Their bills are short and dark and they have yellowish-orange legs.

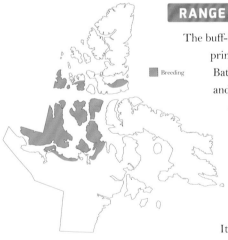

Breeding

RANGE

The buff-breasted sandpiper is a High Arctic species, breeding principally between 66°N and 76°N. It is found on Melville, Bathurst, Devon, Victoria, Jenny Lind, Prince of Wales, and Somerset Islands, and around the Boothia Peninsula. It spends the winter in southern South America.

HABITAT

This species tends to be found in dry, sloping, vegetated tundra or areas with polygon ground with raised ridges, more typical of upland tundra. It forages in grasslands and open areas near wetlands in the winter.

DIET

Omnivore. These shorebirds eat terrestrial insects and spiders, as well as seeds.

REPRODUCTION

The buff-breasted sandpiper is the only North American sandpiper that has a lek mating system. Males defend a small territory and advertise to attract mates. The female chooses a male, mates with him, and then flies off to lay her eggs. Consequently, the female chooses the nest site—often a moss hummock—scrapes and builds the nest, and lays four pale, brownish-green eggs covered with brown blotches. The female incubates the clutch and rears the chicks.

BEHAVIOUR

As a lekking species, male buff-breasted sandpipers need to attract females. Among their repertoire are "flutter jumps," which see them leaping into the air and snapping their wings downward, and "wing ups," which involve a male raising one or both wings vertically to show his position by displaying his bright white underwings. Females choose to mate with males based on the quality of their displays. These sandpipers also exhibit distraction displays when predators are near their nests.

RESEARCH AND MONITORING

Buff-breasted sandpipers have been studied on Victoria Island, and are counted in the regional shorebird surveys that occur intermittently in different parts of Nunavut.

SURVIVAL AND STATUS

There are an estimated 30,000 of these birds in North America, making it one of our most uncommon sandpipers, and their population is declining. Foxes, falcons, gulls, ravens, and jaegers are all predators of sandpipers.

DID YOU KNOW?

Commercial hunting in the 1800s and early 1900s along with habitat change in the migration and wintering grounds led to a major decline in the population of this species. It may once have numbered in the millions.

Dunlin

INUKTITUT NAME
Tuaggaajuq

FRENCH NAME
Béccasseau variable

SCIENTIFIC NAME
Calidris alpina (subspecies *arcticola, hudsonia, pacifica*)

PHOTO: JIM RICHARDS

APPEARANCE

Monomorphic. Dunlins are small shorebirds that weigh 48 to 64 grams and have wingspans of up to 40 centimetres. During the breeding season, dunlins are unmistakable. Their heads, throats, and breasts are whitish but covered with fine, dark brown or black streaks, and their undertails are white. Their backs have obvious rich, reddish-brown feathers interspersed with black dots, and their wings are grey. Most distinctive are the large, squarish black patches on their bellies. They have blackish-green legs and black, slightly downturned bills.

RANGE

Breeding

Dunlins breed in the Low and High Arctic, generally south of 70°N. This includes the Nunavut mainland in the northern Kivalliq region, the Melville and Boothia peninsulas, Southampton and Coats Islands, the islands in Foxe Basin, and southern Baffin Island. They spend the winter along the Pacific and Atlantic coastlines of the United States and northern Mexico.

HABITAT

This shorebird nests primarily in moist, low tundra along the coast. It forages along the edges of pools and tundra wetlands, ponds, and lakes. During migration and in the winter, it is most commonly found along marine mudflats and the muddy or sandy edges of freshwater bodies, as well as in flooded fields.

DIET

Carnivore. These shorebirds eat freshwater and marine crustaceans, mollusks, and worms, as well as terrestrial insects and spiders. They will occasionally eat seeds.

REPRODUCTION

Male dunlins establish territories and make several nest scrapes, from which the female chooses one, then lines it with grasses and leaves and lays four olive to blue-green eggs covered with small splotches and swirls of light brown to black. Both the male and the female take turns incubating the nest and rearing the chicks, although the male assumes more chick-rearing duties as the brood gets older.

PHOTO: JENNIE RAUSCH

BEHAVIOUR

These birds are gregarious during migration and in the winter, sometimes being observed in flocks of thousands on coastal mudflats, often mixed with other sandpiper species. However, they are not social during the breeding season.

PHOTO: MARK MALLORY

RESEARCH AND MONITORING

Dunlins are counted as part of the regional shorebird surveys that occur intermittently in different parts of Nunavut.

SURVIVAL AND STATUS

The dunlin is an abundant shorebird—the North American population is estimated at 1.5 million birds, of which 225,000 (*C. a. hudsonia*) come from Nunavut. Collectively, North American dunlin populations appear to be in decline. Arctic foxes, ravens, gulls, and jaegers may depredate dunlins and their nests, and falcons may catch adult dunlins.

DID YOU KNOW?

The dunlin is one of the most broadly distributed shorebird species around the circumpolar world, and is one of the most studied shorebirds—except in Canada!

Red-necked Phalarope

INUKTITUT NAME
Naluumasortoq

FRENCH NAME
Phalarope à bec étroit

SCIENTIFIC NAME
Phalaropus lobatus

PHOTO: MARK MALLORY

APPEARANCE

Dimorphic. This phalarope is a small, dainty shorebird that weighs 32 to 40 grams and has a wingspan of 40 centimetres. The female is larger and brighter than the male. During the breeding season, the female has a dark greyish-black head, neck, and breast, with dark grey wings, back, rump, and tail. She has a bright white chin and eye patch, and very distinctive, chestnut-red feathers sweeping from the side of the head to the breast. Her underparts are greyish white and mottled. Her bill is thin and black, her legs are dark grey, and her toes are distinctively lobed. The male is similar but paler and duller all over.

RANGE

Red-necked phalaropes are widespread across the Subarctic and Low Arctic, generally south of 70°N. They are found across the Nunavut mainland, the islands in Hudson Bay and Foxe Basin, Baffin Island, and southern Victoria Island. Birds breeding in the western Arctic spend the winter offshore from Mexico south along the coast of South America. The wintering area of eastern Arctic birds is largely unknown.

Breeding

HABITAT

Phalaropes are birds of moist tundra. They nest in vegetation near lakes, pools, bogs, marshes, streams, and low-centred polygon ground, and may nest inland and at altitude. They feed in swimming-depth water in small ponds, as well as in marine waters. During migration, they feed in bays, estuaries, and offshore upwellings and convergence zones.

DIET

Carnivore. Phalaropes eat aquatic insects and their larvae in freshwater, as well as marine crustaceans and worms, and very occasionally small fish.

REPRODUCTION

Phalaropes have opposite sex roles for parts of their reproduction (sex-role reversal), whereby the female lays the eggs but the male does the rest, and the female may mate and lay eggs with more than one male (polyandry). The nest is a small depression in mossy vegetation near a pond, and there the female lays four olive-green eggs with brown speckling. The male then immediately undertakes all incubation and chick-rearing duties, and the female abandons the male to join a flock.

BEHAVIOUR

Phalaropes are highly gregarious throughout the year, and do not exhibit strong territoriality when they nest. You rarely see one phalarope alone, and they may occur in flocks of more than a million on the water. Females may compete viciously for mates. Phalaropes are probably best known for their feeding habit of swimming and then spinning like tops in the water to corral tiny plankton on which to feed.

PHOTO: MARK MALLORY

RESEARCH AND MONITORING

Breeding counts of red-necked phalaropes are recorded in regional shorebird surveys, and there has been specific research on their biology on Southampton Island and Coats Island.

SURVIVAL AND STATUS

There are probably more than 2.5 million red-necked phalaropes in Canada, hundreds of thousands of which breed in Nunavut. However, there have been dramatic declines in the counts of these phalaropes in eastern Canada. Phalaropes and their nests are hunted by Arctic foxes, falcons, gulls, ravens, and jaegers.

LOCAL ECOLOGICAL KNOWLEDGE

Traditionally, Inuit would keep the skin of a phalarope in their kayaks. If the water got rough, they would throw the skin in the water, as they believed it would calm the waves, preventing them from getting lost.

DID YOU KNOW?

Red-necked phalaropes used to be seen in flocks of millions in the Bay of Fundy in eastern Canada, but these have largely disappeared. It is unclear whether the population has declined or the birds have moved their migration route. A similar, dramatic decline has occurred in phalaropes that winter off the coast of Japan.

PHOTO: CAMERON ECKERT

FAMILY SCOLOPACIDAE

Red Phalarope

INUKTITUT NAME
Shutgak; Kajuaraq

FRENCH NAME
Phalarope à bec large

SCIENTIFIC NAME
Phalaropus fulicarius

APPEARANCE

Dimorphic. This small shorebird weighs 49 to 62 grams and has a wingspan of 44 centimetres. The female is larger and brighter than the male. During the breeding season, the female has a distinctive, bright, chestnut-red neck and underparts, a black crown, and white cheek patches. Her back and wings are blackish with bold, tan-coloured fringing, making the back look streaked. The upper wings are dark grey and the underwings are white. She has a bright yellow bill and yellowish-brown legs, with lobed toes. The male is similar but paler and duller than the female, and in particular his crown is brown with black streaks.

RANGE

Breeding

Red phalaropes are more marine than red-necked phalaropes, and they are commonly found in the High Arctic, north of 70°N. They occur along southern Baffin Island, the islands in Hudson Bay and Foxe Basin, the mainland (Kivalliq region) along western Hudson Bay, and all of the High Arctic islands, except in the northwest (Ellef and Amund Ringnes Islands). They winter off the western coast of Africa and both coasts of South America.

HABITAT

Phalaropes are birds of moist tundra. They nest in vegetation near lakes, pools, bogs, marshes, streams, and low-centred polygon ground, and may nest inland and at altitude. They feed in the shallow, wading-depth parts of small ponds, as well as in marine waters. During migration they feed in bays, estuaries, and offshore upwellings and convergence zones.

DIET

Carnivore. Phalaropes eat tiny adult and larval aquatic insects and crustaceans. They add minute zooplankton to their diet during migration and in the winter.

REPRODUCTION

Phalaropes have opposite sex roles for parts of their reproduction (sex-role reversal), whereby the female lays the eggs but the male does the rest, and the female may mate and lay eggs with more than one male (polyandry). The nest is a small depression in sedge vegetation near a pond, often tall enough for some of the plants to be pulled over the nest like a canopy. The female lays four olive-green eggs with brown speckling. The male then immediately undertakes all incubation and chick-rearing duties, and the female abandons the male to join a flock.

PHOTO: JIM RICHARDS

BEHAVIOUR

Phalaropes are highly gregarious throughout the year, and do not exhibit strong territoriality when they nest. Red phalaropes may nest in high densities of up to 64 birds per square kilometre, with nests only five metres apart in suitable habitats. Females may compete viciously for mates during the breeding season. Phalaropes are probably best known for their feeding habit of swimming and then spinning like tops in the water to corral tiny plankton on which to feed.

RESEARCH AND MONITORING

Breeding counts of red phalaropes are recorded in regional shorebird surveys, and research on their breeding biology has been undertaken on Bathurst Island.

SURVIVAL AND STATUS

There is a rough estimate of 1.3 million red phalaropes in North America, many from Nunavut, and scientists agree that their population is declining. Arctic foxes, falcons, gulls, ravens, and jaegers hunt phalaropes and their nests.

PHOTO: MARK MALLORY

DID YOU KNOW?

Red phalaropes have a habit of feeding near whales when the mammals stir up mud, with its associated tiny crustaceans. This prompted European whalers to call them *bowhead birds* and use them to locate whales.

FAMILY LARIDAE

Black-legged Kittiwake

INUKTITUT NAME
Tiratiraaq; taateraaq

FRENCH NAME
Mouette tridactyle

SCIENTIFIC NAME
Rissa tridactyla

PHOTO: MARK MALLORY

APPEARANCE

Monomorphic. The kittiwake is a small, graceful gull weighing up to 580 grams, with a wingspan of up to 120 centimetres. It has a white head, throat, breast, and underside. Its back and wings are light grey with distinct black wingtips. It has a yellow bill and black legs.

■ Breeding

RANGE

Kittiwakes are common in marine areas in northern Baffin Bay, Lancaster Sound, along the east coast of Baffin Island, and in the waters at the eastern entrance to Hudson Strait. They are not found in Hudson Bay or Foxe Basin in appreciable numbers. In the winter they inhabit the Labrador Sea between Greenland and Newfoundland and Labrador.

HABITAT

This is truly a marine gull—you do not find kittiwakes at garbage dumps. They nest on narrow ledges of steep cliffs overlooking the ocean, at elevations generally up to 300 metres. During the breeding season, they forage within 30 kilometres of their colonies. In winter they may be found much farther offshore.

DIET

Carnivore. Kittiwakes feed on small fish and zooplankton at the ocean's surface.

REPRODUCTION

Black-legged kittiwake colonies range from a few dozen to thousands of birds. They build nests of moss, dead vegetation, and mud on their cliff ledges, often adding to or building up nests from previous years. They lay one to three beige-olive, speckled eggs. Males and females share incubation and chick-rearing responsibilities.

BEHAVIOUR

These gulls are gregarious throughout the year, nesting, feeding, migrating, and wintering together in small to large aggregations. In years when sea ice is extensive and late, kittiwakes may lay fewer eggs.

RESEARCH AND MONITORING

Black-legged kittiwakes have been studied at Prince Leopold Island, and colony monitoring occurs at sites around Lancaster Sound and Barrow Strait. Kittiwake eggs are used to monitor contaminant levels in the High Arctic environment.

SURVIVAL AND STATUS

Kittiwakes are locally common. There are probably more than 300,000 kittiwakes in Nunavut, although birds have not been counted at the main colonies in several decades. The number of birds attending colonies in the High Arctic has been increasing since the 1990s. Falcons, eagles, glaucous gulls, and Arctic foxes hunt kittiwakes and their nests.

LOCAL ECOLOGICAL KNOWLEDGE

Interviews in Pond Inlet have suggested that kittiwakes have been taking over breeding ledges at Cape Graham Moore that were occupied mostly by murres.

PHOTO: MARK MALLORY

DID YOU KNOW?
Black-legged kittiwakes are one of three bird species that have been observed very close to the North Pole.

PHOTO: MARK MALLORY

PHOTO: MARK MALLORY

FAMILY LARIDAE
Ivory Gull

INUKTITUT NAME
Nauyavak

FRENCH NAME
Mouette blanche

SCIENTIFIC NAME
Pagophila eburnea

APPEARANCE

Monomorphic. This is a medium-sized gull, weighing 450 to 700 grams (the males being slightly larger than the females). Its wingspan is about 94 centimetres. This is the only gull that has pure white feathers over its entire body. Its bill is dark olive-green with a light tip, and its legs are black. Young, immature birds have black spots on their white feathers.

RANGE

Breeding
Winter

Ivory gulls are High Arctic specialists in the breeding season, being found on the Brodeur Peninsula of northern Baffin Island, Seymour Island, Devon Island, and eastern Ellesmere Island. In the winter they move to the edge of the pack ice in Davis Strait and down along coastal Labrador.

HABITAT

This gull nests in two strikingly different habitats. Some nest on isolated, rocky islands or remote, flat limestone plateaus, but most of the surviving Canadian population breed on steep cliffs surrounded by glaciers (*nunataks*) at elevations of up to 1,600 metres above sea level. They are usually found near ice—they breed near glaciers, use icebergs as perches, and feed along the floe edge, in leads in the ice, or on pack ice. Most spend the winter offshore in the pack ice, although some may be observed closer to shore and occasionally at garbage dumps.

DIET

Carnivore and scavenger. Ivory gulls are very adept at finding marine mammal carcasses to scavenge, probably by following polar bears or Inuit hunters. They also catch fish and zooplankton, and will feed at human dumps if they are near coastlines.

REPRODUCTION

Ivory gulls nest in small colonies of up to 200 breeding pairs. They build nests of moss and dead vegetation, and lay one to three olive-green eggs covered with pale, irregular brown splotches. The male and the female share incubation and chick-rearing duties, and defend their nests strongly from all intruders and predators.

PHOTO: MARK MALLORY

BEHAVIOUR

These gulls are gregarious during breeding, nesting in small colonies, and may be observed in small flocks during winter and migration. Away from the colony, they are often solitary, unless there is an abundant food supply. Interestingly, island-nesting ivory gulls share their breeding sites with other species, such as terns, brant, and eiders, but those nesting on *nunataks* are remote from all other breeding birds. Ivory gulls are very tame, and will land and try to steal fat from seals killed by polar bears or Inuit hunters.

RESEARCH AND MONITORING

Ivory gulls have been studied at Seymour Island Migratory Bird Sanctuary, and since 2002 most of their known breeding areas are surveyed every few years to monitor their population size.

SURVIVAL AND STATUS

The number of ivory gulls in Canada has dropped by more than 70% at traditional colonies since the 1980s, and less than 700 birds were counted in the last complete survey of all known colonies in 2009. This gull is listed as endangered by COSEWIC and is also listed under the federal *Species at Risk Act*. The reason for the species' sudden decline remains unknown. Ivory gulls nest apart from most other vertebrates, but for ground-nesting colonies, their nests are susceptible to polar bear and Arctic fox predation. Glaucous gulls and falcons may attack adults and young ivory gulls.

LOCAL ECOLOGICAL KNOWLEDGE

Territorial conservation officers and Inuit hunters first alerted scientists to the apparent decline in the ivory gull population. During interviews in High Arctic communities, hunters and elders indicated that they used to see ivory gulls in the spring scavenging marine mammal carcasses that had been butchered out on the ice in front of their communities. Some people said there were so many gulls and they were so loud that it was hard to sleep! In recent years, people have only seen ravens and larger gulls at these carcasses.

DID YOU KNOW?

Because they scavenge marine mammal carcasses, ivory gulls and their eggs have some of the highest concentrations of contaminants of any birds in Nunavut. In particular, eggs from some ivory gulls at Seymour Island have the highest mercury concentrations found in any marine bird eggs in the circumpolar Arctic.

FAMILY LARIDAE
Sabine's Gull

INUKTITUT NAME
Iqiggagiarjuk; igaqgagiaq

FRENCH NAME
Mouette de Sabine

SCIENTIFIC NAME
Xema sabini

APPEARANCE

Monomorphic. This is a small gull, weighing 170 to 200 grams, with males being slightly larger than the females. Its wingspan is up to 90 centimetres. In the breeding season, it has a dark grey head, a black collar around its neck, and a white neck and breast. The Sabine's gull has a grey back and a distinctive, three-coloured upperwing composed of an outer black triangle, middle white triangle, and inner grey triangle. In flight, its tail is forked, which is also distinctive. Its bill is black with a yellow tip, its legs are dusky grey with brownish webs, and its inner mouth is a brilliant red. It has narrow red rings around its eyes.

RANGE

Breeding

Sabine's gulls are found mostly in the High Arctic, north of 64°N—in northern mainland areas along Queen Maud Gulf, around the Boothia Peninsula, on small islands in Queen's Channel and Foxe Basin, and on Victoria, Somerset, Bylot, and western Baffin islands. In the winter, Sabine's gulls move along coastlines to marine areas off western Africa or western South America.

HABITAT

This gull nests on moist ground along coastal tundra, near freshwater pools, lakes, tidal marshes, or low coastal islands, and is often associated with Arctic tern colonies. It feeds in freshwater ponds, coastal wetlands, and lowlands (and less commonly in marine areas during the breeding season). During migration and in the winter, it feeds along marine coastlines or offshore over convergence zones and upwellings.

DIET

Carnivore. These gulls eat terrestrial and aquatic insects and spiders during breeding, but they switch to a marine diet of zooplankton, crustaceans, and fish during migration and in the winter.

REPRODUCTION

Sabine's gulls nest in small colonies. They lay one to three olive-green eggs covered with pale, irregular brown splotches. The male and female share incubation and chick-rearing duties, and defend their nests strongly from all intruders and predators.

PHOTO: MARK MALLORY

BEHAVIOUR

These gulls are gregarious during the winter and migration and are often seen in flocks of up to 2,000 birds. During the breeding season they are less gregarious and are very territorial around their nest sites. They exhibit a diverse array of postures and calls that signal their intentions to other birds (e.g., aggression, submission, courtship).

RESEARCH AND MONITORING

Sabine's gulls are counted during different types of regional bird surveys, and have been studied intensively on Southampton Island and on islands in Queen's Channel in the High Arctic.

PHOTO: MARK MALLORY

SURVIVAL AND STATUS

There are no estimates for the size of the Sabine's gull population in Nunavut, although it probably numbers in the tens of thousands. Trends in the population are also unknown. Gull chicks and eggs are eaten by foxes, gulls, ravens, and jaegers, and adult birds are hunted by falcons, eagles, and owls.

PHOTO: MARK MALLORY

DID YOU KNOW?

Sabine's gulls are the only gulls from Nunavut known to exhibit trans-equatorial migration, meaning that they must fly at least 20,000 kilometres round trip between their wintering and breeding grounds each year.

FAMILY LARIDAE

Ross's Gull

INUKTITUT NAME
Nasaruvaalik

FRENCH NAME
Mouette rosée

SCIENTIFIC NAME
Rhodostethia rosea

PHOTO: MARK MALLORY

APPEARANCE

Monomorphic. This is a small gull, weighing about 200 grams, with a wingspan of about 84 centimetres. Adults have white heads, necks, breasts, and undersides, with pale grey backs, wings, and tails. In many birds, the white plumage is tinted pale to bright pink. The gull is distinctive as it has a wedge-shaped tail. The bill is black and the feet are bright reddish orange.

Breeding Only

RANGE

Ross's gulls are very rare, but colonies have been found on islands in Foxe Basin and Queen's Channel. Ross's gulls are observed in flocks near Alaska in the late fall, suggesting that birds from Nunavut may migrate west for the winter.

HABITAT

In Nunavut, all known Ross's gull colonies have been co-located with Arctic tern colonies, on small, flat islands near the coastline. In the High Arctic, these habitats are usually low gravel islands, but farther south, near Churchill, as well as in Siberia, Russia (where most are known to breed), they nest in more vegetated tundra near rivers and coasts. Their wintering habitats are largely unknown, although they have been encountered at sea near Alaska and Russia in the early winter.

DIET

Carnivore. Ross's gulls feed mostly on small fish and zooplankton around ice and near coastlines.

REPRODUCTION

Little known. Colonies that have been found in Canada are always smaller than seven nests. In their nests—typically rounded scrapes in the ground—they lay one to three olive-green eggs covered with pale, irregular brown splotches. The male and female share incubation and chick-rearing duties, and defend their nests from intruders. Unlike terns and Sabine's gulls, however, Ross's gulls leave their nests while threats are still far away, presumably to minimize the chance that predators will see them sitting on the ground.

BEHAVIOUR

PHOTO: MARK MALLORY

These gulls are gregarious during breeding, nesting in small colonies, but can be seen in flocks of thousands during migration. They are usually found breeding in association with Arctic terns and Sabine's gulls, but this may be simply because all three species prefer the same type of breeding habitat.

RESEARCH AND MONITORING

The first Ross's gull breeding site in North America was discovered at the Cheyne Islands in the 1970s, and since then only four other breeding locations have been reported anywhere on the continent.

SURVIVAL AND STATUS

Ross's gulls are probably the rarest breeding gull in North America. We do not know how many Ross's gulls live and breed in Nunavut, but it may be less than 100. Less than ten nests are known each year, but Ross's gulls may breed in areas where people don't go. This gull is listed as threatened by COSEWIC and is also listed under the federal *Species at Risk Act*. Ross's gull nests have been depredated by Arctic foxes, and are susceptible to gull, raven, and jaeger predation.

PHOTO: MARK MALLORY

LOCAL ECOLOGICAL KNOWLEDGE

Surveys in communities of southern Baffin Island indicated that many hunters were familiar with Ross's gulls, even though none of these birds appear to breed near there. This suggests that either non-breeding birds feed or migrate along coastlines in this region, or that there are small colonies of gulls breeding somewhere along Foxe Basin or Hudson Bay, as yet undiscovered.

DID YOU KNOW?

When they are flying near their colonies, trying to distract predators from their nests, they make calls that sound like the squeaky toys people have for their pet dogs!

FAMILY LARIDAE

Iceland Gull

INUKTITUT NAME
Naujaq

FRENCH NAME
Goéland arctique

SCIENTIFIC NAME
Larus glaucoides

APPEARANCE

Monomorphic. This medium-sized gull weighs 800 to 1,100 grams and has a wingspan sometimes extending to 150 centimetres. Adults have white heads, necks, breasts, and undersides, with very pale grey backs, wings, and tails. In bright light, these birds often appear white. Their feet are pinkish and their bills are yellow. They resemble glaucous gulls except that they are smaller, slimmer, and have rounder heads.

Breeding Only

RANGE

Iceland gulls are common around southeastern Baffin Island and islands in Hudson Strait. In the winter, they migrate to Newfoundland and Labrador and coastal Greenland.

HABITAT

These gulls nest on steep cliff faces over the ocean along rocky, mountainous coastlines. They generally feed along coastal areas at sea, but some will forage in community dumps. Their wintering habitats are similar—principally rocky coastal areas where they can hunt and scavenge.

DIET

Carnivore and scavenger. Iceland gulls typically feed on small fish, as well as mollusks and zooplankton, but they will also scavenge fish and marine mammal carcasses. As well, they eat many types of refuse at community dumps.

REPRODUCTION

Iceland gulls nest in colonies of up to 100 pairs, choosing cliff faces up to 300 metres high. They build nests from moss and vegetation, and there they lay one to three olive-brown speckled eggs.

Both parents perform incubation and chick-rearing duties, which include strong defense of their nest against any intruders.

BEHAVIOUR

These gulls may nest in association with other seabirds, including thick-billed murres, black-legged kittiwakes, and black guillemots, but their nests are usually segregated on cliffs, away from these other species.

RESEARCH AND MONITORING

Iceland gulls have been the subject of minimal study, except for some work in Home Bay near Clyde River.

SURVIVAL AND STATUS

Iceland gulls have not been surveyed regularly, but scientists estimate that there are 60,000 of them in Nunavut. There is no information on whether their population size is changing. Foxes, glaucous gulls, ravens, and falcons may all be significant predators of Iceland gulls.

PHOTO: MARK MALLORY

DID YOU KNOW?

Despite their nest defense, Iceland gulls may undertake "panic flights," where virtually all of the birds on their nests will depart the colony at the same time, returning a short time later. These often occur when one or more gulls detect certain predators approaching quickly (often falcons), or if birds hear certain noises, like rock falls.

PHOTO: MARK MALLORY

FAMILY LARIDAE

Glaucous Gull

INUKTITUT NAME
Naujaq; najavigjuaq

FRENCH NAME
Goéland bourgemestre

SCIENTIFIC NAME
Larus hyperboreus

APPEARANCE

Monomorphic. This is a large, powerful gull weighing 1.2 to 2.7 kilograms. It is the largest gull in Nunavut (the male is larger than the female), and has a broad wingspan extending up to 180 centimetres. Adults have white heads, necks, breasts, and undersides, with very pale grey backs, wings, and tails. In bright light, these birds often appear white. Their feet are pinkish and their bills are yellow. Their heads are angular rather than rounded.

Breeding
Breeding and winter
Winter

RANGE

Glaucous gulls are common but dispersed across coastal areas of the High Arctic, south to approximately 62°N (northern Hudson Bay), although non-breeders are found south of there. In the winter, they migrate west to coastal Alaska or east to Greenland or Newfoundland and Labrador.

HABITAT

These gulls are most commonly associated with nesting on rock stacks or cliff ledges along rocky Arctic coastlines, but they also nest on beaches, cliffs along inland rivers, and low islands of freshwater lakes close to marine coastlines. They generally feed along coastal areas, but some individuals head to sea to forage, and others feed inland, particularly if they are nesting in an area that supports other species, like nesting geese. Their wintering habitats are similar, and include rocky coastal areas where they can hunt and scavenge.

DIET

Carnivore and scavenger. At seabird colonies, glaucous gulls consume eggs, chicks, and adults of other seabirds, and sometimes lemmings. When at sea, they catch fish or marine invertebrates, but also scavenge fish, fisheries' discards from boats, and marine mammal carcasses. They are commonly observed feeding in community dumps, where they will eat almost anything.

REPRODUCTION

Glaucous gulls nest solitarily, although there may be several nests along the same cliff face, island, or beach. They build large nests from moss and vegetation, and lay one to three large, olive eggs covered with dark brown speckles there. Both parents perform incubation and chick-rearing duties. These gulls defend their nests fiercely. Scientists usually wear helmets to work near their nests for any prolonged period of time.

BEHAVIOUR

These gulls are usually observed solitarily or in pairs along the coast, unless there is an abundant food supply (e.g. in a dump), in which case they can occur in tens or hundreds of birds.

PHOTO: MARK MALLORY

RESEARCH AND MONITORING

Glaucous gull research has often been undertaken along with other seabird or goose work, in order to learn how predation by these gulls affects other birds. Major studies on glaucous gulls have been undertaken at Queen Maud Gulf Migratory Bird Sanctuary, and on Prince Leopold, Coats, and northern Devon Islands.

SURVIVAL AND STATUS

Glaucous gulls are common across Nunavut, although they rarely occur in large numbers. Scientists estimate that there are probably 25,000 glaucous gulls in the Canadian Arctic (mostly in Nunavut). There is concern, however, that gulls are declining near some seabird colonies where they used to be more common. Glaucous gulls have few natural predators, but their nests may be depredated by foxes or bears.

LOCAL ECOLOGICAL KNOWLEDGE

Surveys in communities around Nunavut have indicated that Inuit see more "large" gulls (most of which are glaucous gulls) around communities than they did in the past. This is probably a result of greater amounts of garbage for gulls to feed on today than when communities were first established.

DID YOU KNOW?

Glaucous gulls are top marine predators and are one of the key birds used to monitor contaminant levels all around the Arctic.

FAMILY LARIDAE

Arctic Tern

INUKTITUT NAME
Immiqutailaq; tikatikiaq

FRENCH NAME
Sterne arctique

SCIENTIFIC NAME
Sterna paradisaea

PHOTO: MARK MALLORY

APPEARANCE

Monomorphic. This small, tapered, elegant seabird weighs 100 grams and has a wingspan of about 75 centimetres. Adults have black caps, grey backs and wings, and white cheeks, throats, breasts, and bellies. Their tails are white and deeply forked. Their legs and bills are both a brilliant shade of reddish orange, though their legs are very short and their bills are long and narrow. Their wings are relatively long and pointed.

Breeding

RANGE

Arctic terns are widespread across all of Nunavut, with the exception of some of the northwestern islands (e.g., Borden Island). In the winter, they migrate south through the Atlantic Ocean and along the western coast of Africa, spending the winter near Antarctica.

HABITAT

Arctic terns nest on low gravel islands or peninsulas near the ocean, or occasionally on gravel islands in freshwater lakes, usually near the coast. They feed near the shore—generally within 30 kilometres of their colonies during the breeding season—but some may also forage on the tundra. During migration and in the winter, Arctic terns spend all of their time on the ocean, around coastal Antarctica.

DIET

Carnivore. Arctic terns feed on small fish, zooplankton, and marine worms, taking them from within one metre of the water's surface. Some terns feed on terrestrial insects and spiders.

REPRODUCTION

Terns may nest in high densities in their colonies, although generally there are several metres between nests. These nests are scrapes in the ground, occasionally lined with bits of lichen or vegetation, in which the female lays one or two olive-green, speckled eggs. The parents share incubation and chick-rearing duties.

BEHAVIOUR

Terns are highly gregarious throughout the year, nesting in small to large colonies, feeding together at sea, and migrating and wintering in large, loose flocks. Tern colonies exhibit very intense group nest defense, such that many adults will attack intruding birds, mammals, or scientists. Terns chase other birds away, and strike mammals and people with their sharp bills, hard enough to draw blood. Terns can kill lemmings that enter their colonies. The Arctic tern is one of the few birds with the ability to hover like a helicopter, holding itself in one spot in the air to focus on its target.

RESEARCH AND MONITORING

Specific research on terns has been conducted on Southampton Island and on small islands in Queen's Channel. Breeding counts of Arctic terns are recorded in some surveys for other types of birds.

SURVIVAL AND STATUS

There are probably many more Arctic terns breeding in Nunavut than have been found, but it is estimated that there are at least 174,000 terns breeding in the territory. Surveys in some areas suggest that the tern population may be reduced now, compared to what it was in the past. In some areas, Inuit consume many tern eggs if ice conditions allow them to reach the colonies before the eggs are too developed. Foxes, bears, gulls, ravens, and jaegers prey on tern nests and young, and falcons kill tern adults.

LOCAL ECOLOGICAL KNOWLEDGE

Knowledge from some regions suggests that Arctic tern numbers are in decline, particularly along the western coast of Hudson Bay.

DID YOU KNOW?

Arctic terns have the distinction of having the longest migration of any bird known—more than 80,000 kilometres each year. Because they are in the Arctic in our summer and the Antarctic during our winter, they see more daylight than any other animal.

PHOTO: MARK MALLORY

FAMILY LARIDAE

Pomarine Jaeger

INUKTITUT NAME
Isunngarluk

FRENCH NAME
Labbe pomarin

SCIENTIFIC NAME
Stercorarius pomarinus

PHOTO: MARK MALLORY

APPEARANCE

Sexually monomorphic, although females slightly larger than males. This is a large, powerfully built seabird that weighs 500 to 1,000 grams and has a wingspan of 120 centimetres, making it the largest of the three jaegers. It has long, pointed wings and two central tail feathers that extend beyond most of the tail. The pomarine's tail feathers have a twist and are rounded, which makes them look a bit like two spoons. These birds occur in two colour morphs. The less common dark morph is a uniform, slatish brown, with a darker tail and cap on its head, lighter cheeks, a black, hooked bill, and black legs. The more common light morph has a dark brownish-black cap and tail, brown wings, a white underside with a brown band across the breast, a brown back, and pale, creamy-yellow cheeks and nape. The underside of the primary feathers has an obvious whitish patch.

Breeding

RANGE

This jaeger has a more restricted range than other jaegers, generally being found between 65°N and 75°N. They are known to nest on Southampton, Victoria, Bathurst, and Somerset Islands. They are commonly observed on other High Arctic islands, but breeding in those locations has not been confirmed. In the winter these birds can be found around the Caribbean islands and offshore of coastal South America.

HABITAT

Pomarine jaegers nest in low-lying, marshy tundra or sedge meadows, often near lakes, rivers, or coastlines. They forage on the tundra, and less frequently along freshwater or marine coastlines. During migration and in the winter, these jaegers spend all of their time on the ocean.

DIET

Carnivore and kleptoparasite. Pomarine jaegers are lemming specialists during the breeding season, but when they are not breeding, they consume fish and large crustaceans, as well as fisheries' discards and carrion. In the winter, they steal food from other birds.

REPRODUCTION

Most pomarine jaegers nest only in years of lemming abundance, so there are many years when their nests are not found, even in apparently good habitats. They disperse their nests across the tundra, doing so in higher densities (up to ten nests per square kilometre) in years of peak numbers of lemmings. Their nests are simple scrapes in the ground, usually on mounds or slightly higher ridges than their surroundings. In these nests, female pomarines lay two brownish-olive, spotted eggs. The parents share incubation and chick-rearing duties. All jaegers are extremely defensive around their nests and will try to drive other birds and animals away.

BEHAVIOUR

In the breeding season, pomarine jaegers are highly territorial when nesting, but will travel in groups when not breeding. These birds may appear tame, like the other jaegers.

SURVIVAL AND STATUS

Pomarine jaegers are locally common in parts of Nunavut, but they occur at very low densities, so we do not have a good estimate of how many there are, nor do we know whether their population is changing. Jaegers have few natural predators, but their nests are susceptible to fox predation.

LOCAL ECOLOGICAL KNOWLEDGE

Inuit used the skins of jaegers as towels to wipe their hands.

DID YOU KNOW?

All jaegers steal food from other birds, but pomarines are perhaps the scariest. They are powerful and use brute force in encounters, hitting, biting, and clutching their targets until they crash into the water, then holding them underwater until they regurgitate fish for the jaegers to steal.

PHOTO: MARK MALLORY

FAMILY LARIDAE

Parasitic Jaeger

INUKTITUT NAME
Isunngaq

FRENCH NAME
Labbe parasite

SCIENTIFIC NAME
Stercorarius parasitica

APPEARANCE

Sexually monomorphic, although females slightly larger than males. These medium-sized seabirds look a bit like falcons in flight, with long, pointed wings and two central tail feathers that extend beyond most of the tail. They weigh 380 to 510 grams, and have wingspans of up to 110 centimetres. They occur in two colour morphs. The less common dark morph is a uniform, slatish brown, with a darker tail and cap on the head, lighter cheeks, a black, hooked bill, and black legs. The more common light morph has a dark brownish-black cap and tail, brown wings, and a white underside with a brown band across the breast. It also has a brown back, with pale, creamy-yellow cheeks and nape. On both morphs the outer five or six primary feathers have obvious white shafts.

Breeding

RANGE

In Nunavut, parasitic jaegers spend most of the breeding season feeding on bird eggs or lemmings on the tundra, but during migration and in the winter they spend almost all of their time at sea. This jaeger may be found from southern James Bay to northern Devon Island, from the barrens of central Nunavut to the High Arctic coastlines. They spend the winter at varying distances from coastlines extending from Africa to Australia.

HABITAT

Parasitic jaegers nest in low-lying, marshy tundra or sedge meadows, often near lakes, rivers, or coastlines, and thus can be found north of the treeline in Nunavut. They forage on the tundra and along freshwater or marine coastlines. During migration and in the winter, these jaegers spend all of their time on the ocean.

DIET

Carnivore and kleptoparasite. Parasitic jaegers eat bird eggs, insects, fish, small birds, and rodents. They also steal food from other birds.

REPRODUCTION

Jaegers disperse their nests across the tundra in very low densities and defend large territories. Their nests are simple scrapes in the ground, and in them, the females lay one or two brownish-olive, spotted eggs. The parents share incubation and chick-rearing duties. Jaegers are extremely defensive around their nests and will try to drive all other birds and animals away from them.

PHOTO: MARK MALLORY

BEHAVIOUR

Jaegers are highly territorial during the breeding season and are usually observed as singles or pairs, though non-breeders may travel together in groups. These birds often appear curious or tame, and will come very close to people or other predators to inspect them. They are highly agile and can almost hover in one place, allowing them to scrutinize intruders. Importantly, their flying skills allow them to follow, harass, and pester other birds (usually seabirds), which causes these birds to drop or regurgitate their food, which the jaeger then steals.

SURVIVAL AND STATUS

Parasitic jaegers are locally common in parts of Nunavut, but they occur at such low densities that scientists do not have a good estimate of how many there are, nor whether their population is changing. Jaegers have few natural predators, but their nests are susceptible to fox predation.

LOCAL ECOLOGICAL KNOWLEDGE

Inuit used the skins of jaegers as towels to wipe their hands.

DID YOU KNOW?

In Europe, this bird is called the Arctic skua, even though the word *jäger* is German for hunter!

PHOTO: MARK MALLORY

FAMILY LARIDAE

Long-tailed Jaeger

INUKTITUT NAME
Isunngaq

FRENCH NAME
Labbe à longue queue

SCIENTIFIC NAME
Stercorarius longicaudus

APPEARANCE

Sexually monomorphic, although females slightly larger than males. This medium-sized seabird is the smallest of the jaegers, weighing 250 to 450 grams and having a wingspan of about 110 centimetres. It is graceful and buoyant in flight, with long, pointed wings and two very long central tail feathers that extend well past the rest of the tail. Unlike other jaegers, adults of this species occur only in a light morph. They have a dark, brownish-black cap and tail, as well as greyish-brown wings, sides, and undertails. They have creamy breasts, necks, and napes, and yellowish cheeks. The key distinctions between this species and the parasitic jaeger are that long-tailed jaegers have long central tail feathers and solid, light-coloured breasts.

RANGE

Breeding

Long-tailed jaegers are the most broadly distributed of the jaegers, occurring anywhere in Nunavut. They spend three-quarters of the year at sea, and in the summer may be found from southern James Bay to northern Devon Island, and from the barren lands of central Nunavut to the High Arctic coastlines. They spend the winter more than 30 kilometres offshore of western Africa, Argentina, or coastal Australia.

HABITAT

These jaegers nest on vegetated tundra north of the treeline, but may choose dry or moist nesting conditions, depending on local habitat conditions. They are often found near small lakes or ponds. They forage primarily on the tundra during peak lemming years, but may feed around freshwater ponds, along marine coastlines, or out at sea in low lemming years. During migration and in the winter, these jaegers spend all of their time on the ocean.

DIET

Carnivore and sometimes omnivore. Unlike other jaegers, long-tailed jaegers are not very proficient at stealing food from other birds, instead hunting for most of their own meals. They specialize in eating lemmings, but will also eat bird eggs, insects, fish, and young birds, and will consume berries throughout the breeding season.

REPRODUCTION

Breeding by long-tailed jaegers is closely tied to the lemming cycle. In years with lots of lemmings, many jaegers will nest and raise young, but in years with no lemmings, long-tailed jaegers will skip breeding. Their nests are simple scrapes in the ground, in which they lay one or two brownish-olive, spotted eggs. The parents share incubation and chick-rearing duties.

BEHAVIOUR

Like other jaegers, this species appears tame and curious and will approach people closely. Long-tailed jaegers are highly territorial and defend their nests vigorously during the breeding season, so they are usually observed as single birds or pairs. In years with no lemmings, these birds may form flocks in early summer. During migration they tend to remain well offshore, and thus are rarely observed, except from ships.

SURVIVAL AND STATUS

Long-tailed jaegers are common in parts of Nunavut, but they occur at very low densities, so scientists do not have a good estimate of how many there are, nor whether their population is changing. Jaegers have few natural predators, but their nests are susceptible to fox predation.

LOCAL ECOLOGICAL KNOWLEDGE

Inuit used the skins of jaegers as towels to wipe their hands.

DID YOU KNOW?

As a trans-equatorial migrant, these birds travel at least 20,000 kilometres round trip each year from their wintering to their breeding grounds.

Dovekie

INUKTITUT NAME
Akpaliarjuq; appaliarsuq

FRENCH NAME
Mergule nain

SCIENTIFIC NAME
Alle alle

PHOTO: CHRISTOPHER GILBER

APPEARANCE

Monomorphic. The dovekie is a tiny, chubby seabird, weighing 150 to 200 grams and having a wingspan of 38 centimetres. It has a rapid, whirring wingbeat, and a short neck and tail. Its head, neck, throat, back, wings, and tail are black, and it has a white chest and underside. Its bill and legs are black. In the winter, the dovekie develops a white chin, throat, and neck.

■ Breeding

RANGE

Dovekies can be found in Baffin Bay, Davis Strait, Lancaster Sound, Jones Sound, and Smith Sound. One breeding colony is known in Canada, at Home Bay between Clyde River and Qikiqtarjuaq on eastern Baffin Island. Dovekies spend the winter offshore from Greenland and Newfoundland and Labrador.

HABITAT

This tiny bird nests in crevices among boulder scree at the one known site in Canada, but also in talus slopes and cliffs in Greenland. They are found offshore from rocky coasts, and among pack ice and leads. During migration and in the winter, they can be found tens to hundreds of kilometres offshore.

DIET

Carnivore. Dovekies are zooplankton specialists, but will also eat small fish and mollusks.

REPRODUCTION

This species may nest in massive colonies, sometimes containing millions of birds. The female lays a single, bluish-green egg on a small bed of pebbles. The male and female both take turns incubating the egg, and both bring food to the chick.

BEHAVIOUR

Dovekies use their wings when diving and can reach depths of 35 metres. During the breeding season, they usually feed within a few kilometres of their colonies, but may travel as far as 100 kilometres.

SURVIVAL AND STATUS

Less than 1,000 dovekies are thought to breed in Canada, but millions migrate through and feed in the waters of the eastern Arctic. Scientists are not sure whether numbers of dovekie in the world are changing because they are very hard to count. Dovekie nests are susceptible to predation by weasels, and their young may be eaten by gulls and ravens. Adult dovekies are also prey for gulls and falcons.

LOCAL ECOLOGICAL KNOWLEDGE

In northwestern Greenland, dovekies were one of the key types of country food traditionally required for Inuit survival. Inuit catch dovekies, place them inside sealskin bags, and leave them to ferment under rocks. Much later, the dovekies are removed and served as a delicacy.

DID YOU KNOW?

Although tiny and referred to as "sea sparrows," dovekies are actually the most abundant seabird in the North Atlantic, numbering anywhere from 30 to 100 million birds!

PHOTO: MARK MALLORY

PHOTO: MARK MALLORY

FAMILY ALCIDAE
Thick-billed Murre

INUKTITUT NAME
Akpa

FRENCH NAME
Marmette de Brünnich; guillemot de Brünnich

SCIENTIFIC NAME
Uria lomvia

APPEARANCE

Monomorphic. Murres are medium-sized, chunky, diving seabirds that weigh about one kilogram and resemble penguins. Their wings are relatively short at approximately 70 centimetres wide. They have black heads, necks, backs, wings, and tails, while their breasts and underbellies are white. Their bills and feet are black, except for a distinctive white stripe near the bases of their upper bills. In the winter, their throat plumage becomes white.

Breeding

Digges Sound

Akpatok Island

RANGE

Murres are found in ten large colonies in Nunavut during the breeding season, spread across the Low and High Arctic. Several of these (Coburg Island, Prince Leopold Island, Cape Hay, Cape Graham Moore, and the Minarets) are protected areas in Nunavut. The largest colonies in Canada (Akpatok Island and Digges Sound) are located in Hudson Strait and northern Hudson Bay. In the winter, most murres move to marine waters off the coast of Newfoundland and Labrador or west Greenland.

HABITAT

Murres nest on narrow ledges on steep cliffs overlooking the ocean, up to 500 metres high. They feed in the pelagic zone, usually within 100 kilometres of their colonies, during the breeding season. However, in the winter they may remain hundreds of kilometres from land.

DIET

Carnivore. Murres are considered primarily piscivorous, largely feeding on Arctic cod during the breeding season, but they also eat other fish like capelin, as well as zooplankton.

REPRODUCTION

Murres nest in colonies with thousands of other murres, and occasionally with fulmars and kittiwakes. The murre's nest is a bare rock ledge on which the female lays a single egg that is usually bluish green with dark brown splotches, although eggs can be almost cream-coloured. If she loses that egg early in the breeding season, she may lay a replacement. Nesting densities can be so high that murres touch each other while incubating. The male and female murres share incubation and chick-rearing duties, but the male departs with the chick during fall migration. The chick jumps from its nest on the cliff to the water below when it is partially grown, and remarkably swims hundreds to thousands of kilometres with its father from the colony to Baffin Bay and Davis Strait and on to the wintering grounds.

BEHAVIOUR

Murres are highly gregarious when in their breeding colonies (up to 1 million birds per colony), when away from their colonies feeding, and during the winter. During migration there can be thousands of murres together near the floe edge. Despite their regular habit of being in groups, disputes can break out in these colonies, which can get very aggressive, occasionally resulting in eggs or chicks being dislodged and tumbling into the ocean. Murres are expert divers, descending

PHOTO: MARK MALLORY

PHOTO: MARK MALLORY

regularly to depths of more than 100 metres (possibly up to 200 metres), and staying underwater for up to three and a half minutes. In contrast, murres have relatively short wings for flying, and consequently must maintain a fast wingbeat to stay in the air.

RESEARCH AND MONITORING

Two of the best-studied colonies of thick-billed murres in the world are on Coats Island and Prince Leopold Island, both in Nunavut. Investigations began there in the mid-1970s and continue today. Other significant investigations were undertaken on Coburg Island, Bylot Island, and Digges Sound. Collectively, these have provided great insights into the behaviour, diet, year-round movements, habitat needs, breeding success, and diving activity of murres. Murre eggs have been studied since 1975 as indicators of contamination levels in the marine environment.

SURVIVAL AND STATUS

The thick-billed murre is the most common seabird in Nunavut, and is found mostly in the Qikiqtani region. There are about 4.3 million murres in Nunavut, and their population appears to be stable. Murres may live up to 30 years. If ice conditions are good for travel, Inuit may harvest thousands of murre eggs in some years. Although only a few hundred adult murres are harvested annually in Nunavut, hundreds of thousands are shot in Newfoundland and Labrador (where they are known as turrs) or in Greenland. Murre eggs and young are prey for glaucous gulls and common ravens, and gyrfalcons prey on adults as well as young murres. Murres are also highly susceptible to human disturbances, as they can be flushed easily from nests by loud noises (like ships), causing many eggs or chicks to die. Many of them are killed in oil spills at sea and they are very susceptible to being caught in gillnets used for fishing.

 ## DID YOU KNOW?

The shape of a murre egg is highly pyriform, with a pointy, narrow end and a fat end. This shape is thought to be an adaptation so that if eggs are disturbed, they tend to roll in a circle back to their starting point rather than rolling off a ledge.

FAMILY ALCIDAE

Black Guillemot

INUKTITUT NAME
Pitseolak

FRENCH NAME
Guillemot à miroir; guillemot noir

SCIENTIFIC NAME
Cepphus grylle

APPEARANCE

Monomorphic. The black guillemot is a small, chunky, diving seabird that weighs up to 450 grams. Its wingspan can be as small as 53 centimetres, which means that it must beat its wings very rapidly when in flight. Its body is entirely black (sometimes with a brownish tinge) except for bright, distinctive white patches on its wings. Its feet and the lining of its bill and mouth are brilliant red. In the winter, its head, neck, underparts, and tail have mostly whitish feathers. Young, immature birds have mottled, silvery feathers.

Breeding

RANGE

Guillemots inhabit coastal areas of eastern Ellesmere, Devon, Bylot, eastern Baffin, and Southampton Islands, the Melville Peninsula, and coastal areas of eastern Hudson Bay and Hudson Strait. The greatest numbers of birds occur in High Arctic waters. Many birds spend the winter among pack ice or along the ice edge, as well as in coastal Greenland and Newfoundland and Labrador.

HABITAT

Black guillemots are common along rocky marine coasts and islands surrounded by shallow waters. They breed in crevices in boulders on cliffs, as well as in holes among the scree and talus slopes below cliffs. During the breeding season they forage, usually within a few kilometres of shore. In winter they use coastal habitats similar to the ones they use during the breeding season, although they may also frequent ice edges and pack ice.

DIET

Carnivore. Guillemots dive for small fish, especially benthic species like blennies, as well as marine invertebrates.

REPRODUCTION

Guillemots nest in small, dispersed colonies of tens to hundreds of birds. The female lays two creamy-white eggs covered with blackish-brown to lilac speckles in a scrape on gravel or bare rock. Both parents share incubation and chick-rearing duties.

BEHAVIOUR

Like the other alcids, guillemots are gregarious in the winter and when in breeding colonies or feeding, although groups are generally small (tens of birds) and the tendency to form social groups is less than in murres. Guillemots use their wings to propel themselves underwater, and may dive up to 50 metres deep. When flying, they move in direct lines, low above the water.

RESEARCH AND MONITORING

Black guillemot breeding biology and diving behaviour have been studied in the islands of Digges Sound in northern Hudson Bay, and their diet has been examined in Lancaster Sound. Guillemot eggs are tested to monitor levels of contaminants in the Arctic marine environment.

PHOTO: MARK MALLORY

SURVIVAL AND STATUS

Black guillemots are very common around marine shorelines in parts of Nunavut, but they are small and dive quickly and discretely, and thus are exceedingly difficult to count. A rough estimate is that there are probably 450,000 black guillemots in Nunavut. A few hundred black guillemot adults and eggs are harvested annually by Inuit in Nunavut. Guillemot eggs may be eaten by weasels and foxes, and adult and young birds may be eaten by owls, falcons, and large gulls.

LOCAL ECOLOGICAL KNOWLEDGE

Inuit used the skins of guillemots as slippers for children, and as towels to wipe their hands.

DID YOU KNOW?

The black guillemot winters farther north than any other seabird in the Canadian Arctic. Some may overwinter in the polynyas and leads in the ice of Hudson Bay, Hudson Strait, and even northern Baffin Bay, up to 79°N.

Snowy Owl

INUKTITUT NAME
Uppijjuaq; ukpigjuaq

FRENCH NAME
Harfang des neiges

SCIENTIFIC NAME
Bubo scandiacus

APPEARANCE

Monomorphic. The snowy owl is a large bird, weighing 1.5 to 3 kilograms (the female being heavier than the male), and having a wingspan of up to 160 centimetres. As adults, they are mostly white, with some black or brown barring on their feathers. They have brilliant yellow eyes, and their yellow bills are hidden among white feathers. Their feet are covered with white feathers, and they have long, conspicuous black talons. Males tend to be paler than females or juveniles.

Breeding Only

RANGE

The snowy owl occurs everywhere in Nunavut, except in the southwest near the treeline. Some spend the winter in Nunavut, while others disperse themselves around flat, open parts of southern Canada and the northern United States. These owls are highly nomadic, so they may breed in a site one year, and the following year could breed thousands of kilometres away, perhaps moving where they think there will be a lot of lemmings.

HABITAT

Snowy owls are found in rolling, hummocky open tundra. They prefer sites with mounds or bluffs on which they can rest and scan for prey or predators. In the winter, they are found in similarly open habitats.

DIET

Carnivore. Snowy owls eat lemmings, other small rodents, Arctic hare, birds, and occasionally fish. One owl can eat 1,600 lemmings in a year.

REPRODUCTION

These owls may skip breeding in years of low food (lemming) supply. The male establishes a territory and the female digs a scrape in the ground, in which she lays three to eleven white or cream-coloured eggs, laying larger clutches in years with lots of lemmings. The female alone incubates while the male guards her and the nest. Both parents help rear the young. They aggressively defend their nests and young, and will attack foxes, wolves, and people who come too close.

BEHAVIOUR

Highly territorial and solitary, owls are unlikely to be seen in groups, except when paired for breeding. Owls have a very distinctive flight; they take several deep, slow, powerful strokes with their wings and then glide. Their feathers are designed to be silent in flight, so they can swoop in on unsuspecting prey. Snowy owls differ from most other owls because they are diurnal (hunting by day), while most others are nocturnal (hunting at night).

RESEARCH AND MONITORING

Snowy owls have been studied on Bylot Island.

PHOTO: JIM RICHARDS

SURVIVAL AND STATUS

Researchers currently lack data on the size of, or trends in, snowy owl populations. Their population is difficult to track because the numbers of owls vary in relation to lemming numbers, and the owls move to new breeding locations between years. Snowy owls have few natural predators, although foxes can destroy their nests.

LOCAL ECOLOGICAL KNOWLEDGE

Young Inuit girls once used the eyes of owls as toy buckets for their wooden dolls to carry.

DID YOU KNOW?

The snowy owl is an iconic Arctic bird, the provincial bird of Québec, and it is commonly associated with white, windswept landscapes.

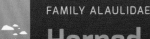

Horned Lark

INUKTITUT NAME
Qaurulligaaq; tingugluktuq

FRENCH NAME
Alouette hausse-col

SCIENTIFIC NAME
Eremophila alpestris

PHOTO: JIM RICHARDS

APPEARANCE

Dimorphic. This small songbird weighs 28 to 40 grams and has a wingspan of 30 centimetres. During the breeding season, the male is brown with darker brown or black streaks on his nape, back, rump, upper tail, and wings. His upper wings are reddish brown, and the outer feathers on the tail are white when he is in flight. His neck, breast, and sides may vary from reddish brown to white. His head, neck, and black upper breast are striking. A black bar runs from his bill to his eye and down, and a black bar on the crown extends to feather tufts on either side of his head, which are held up to look like horns. On his forehead, yellow to white colouring extends back and down, and separates the two black bars. His chin is lemon yellow, and his bill and legs are black. The female has a similar overall pattern, but is clearly lighter, browner, and duller in appearance.

Breeding Only

RANGE

Horned larks may be found anywhere in Nunavut south of 76°N (i.e., south of Ellesmere Island). In the winter they are found mostly in the United States and northern Mexico.

HABITAT

Larks are found year-round in open, dry, barren country, often in gravelly or rocky areas.

DIET

Omnivore. Larks eat various seeds and insects during the summer, and rely on seeds during the winter.

REPRODUCTION

The male lark establishes a territory and the female chooses a nest site within it. She makes a small scrape, usually protected by a clump of grass or a rock, and lines it with vegetation. The female lays two to five tan or ground-coloured eggs that are heavily speckled with darker brown. Only the female incubates, but both parents feed and rear the young.

BEHAVIOUR

Horned larks are territorial during breeding, but gregarious during the winter. They are frequently seen in mixed-species flocks, often with their Arctic neighbours, snow buntings. Horned larks are noted for their beautiful songs, and for enjoying vigorous dust baths.

RESEARCH AND MONITORING

Horned larks have been identified in surveys in many locations across Nunavut, and have been studied at the Truelove Lowlands on Devon Island.

SURVIVAL AND STATUS

There is no estimate for the North American or Nunavut populations of horned larks. The continental population is thought to be stable, although researchers have noticed fewer larks around Iqaluit than in the 1960s. Adult birds are prey for owls and falcons, and their eggs and young may be eaten by foxes, weasels, jaegers, hawks, owls, gulls, and ravens.

PHOTO: MARK MALLORY

FAMILY CORVIDAE
Common Raven

INUKTITUT NAME
Tulugaq

FRENCH NAME
Grand corbeau

SCIENTIFIC NAME
Corvus corax

PHOTO: MARK MALLORY

APPEARANCE

Monomorphic. This is the only large, black landbird in Nunavut. The adults weigh 950 to 1,500 grams, with a wingspan of 140 centimetres, and males are larger than females. All parts of the bird are black.

Resident year-round

RANGE

During the breeding season, ravens are found everywhere in Nunavut except for the northern half of Ellesmere Island. In the winter they are found around all human communities, and occasionally on the sea ice or land south of 70°N. Although they are not considered true migrants, ravens exhibit a general distribution shift south in the winter. The raven is one of the most broadly distributed birds in the northern hemisphere.

HABITAT

Ravens nest on cliff ledges with sheltered overhangs anywhere in their breeding range, and will forage over all available habitats. In the winter, they are now common in all human communities across Nunavut, but will also frequent areas where other wildlife (bears, wolves, and caribou) may leave carcasses or feces for them to scavenge.

DIET

Omnivore. Common ravens eat anything, dead or alive: seeds, berries, insects, marine invertebrates, lemmings, small birds, bird eggs, carcasses, fruit, grains, and human garbage.

REPRODUCTION

Ravens build nests of sticks on cliff ledges, and line the nest cups with vegetation. The male assists in bringing sticks, but the female does most of the nest construction. She lays three to seven (usually five) olive-green to blue eggs speckled with brown. The parents share incubation duties, although the female does most of it, and both parents rear the chicks.

PHOTO: MARK MALLORY

BEHAVIOUR

The common raven is among the most intelligent of birds. Tame and wild birds have been shown to learn quickly, even in new situations, and they have a complex and fantastic repertoire of sounds and calls that they use to communicate with one another. They have good memories, and will bury or store food to retrieve at a later date. Ravens also innovate tools, like dropping clams on rocks to break them open. Ravens remain solitary or in pairs during breeding, but non-breeding birds, birds living near abundant food resources, and birds wintering in Arctic locations can be gregarious and numerous, sometimes gathering in flocks of hundreds. Ravens have many fascinating, curious behaviours. In Iqaluit, they can be seen "playing" with (presumably young) peregrine falcons in the fall, locking feet and tumbling through the air before letting go.

RESEARCH AND MONITORING

Minor aspects of raven biology have been studied when they nest in, or feed at, seabird colonies, but otherwise ravens have received little study in Nunavut.

SURVIVAL AND STATUS

There is no reliable estimate for the number of ravens in Nunavut, although it would likely be in the thousands. Similarly, no one has kept track of raven numbers, but there are probably more now than in the past because many ravens can survive the winter on human garbage. They have few natural predators, although raven eggs are prey for foxes and gulls, and ravens may occasionally be killed by falcons.

LOCAL ECOLOGICAL KNOWLEDGE

Consensus between many communities suggests that there are now more ravens near communities than in the past. In Resolute Bay and Grise Fiord, ravens did not spend the winter there in the early years after community establishment, but now some do.

?

DID YOU KNOW?

In many aboriginal cultures, the raven is known as a trickster and is associated with creating the earth. The raven is also a commonly mentioned animal in poetry and literature, symbolizing wisdom, danger, or death.

PHOTO: DAVID HUSSELL

FAMILY MUSCICAPIDAE

Northern Wheatear

INUKTITUT NAME
Qupanuaq

FRENCH NAME
Traquet motteux

SCIENTIFIC NAME
Oenanthe oenanthe

APPEARANCE

Dimorphic. This is a small songbird that weighs 18 to 33 grams and has a wingspan of up to 32 centimetres. During the breeding season, the male has a blue-grey cap and back; black wings and mask through the eye; white forehead, eyebrows, belly, and underparts; and a black bill and legs. The sides of the throat are often a creamy yellow. The upper tail is white, giving the distinctive appearance of a white rump in flight, while the outer tail is a dark black band. In flight, the black marks on the tail look like an inverted "T." The female has a similar pattern to the male, but is duller and browner overall, often without the distinctive facemask.

Breeding Only

RANGE

Wheatears are found on eastern Baffin Island, southern Ellesmere Island, and sometimes as far west as parts of Hudson Bay. They spend the winter in Africa.

HABITAT

This songbird is common in dry, rocky areas and on open, mountainous tundra. They nest in crevices and cavities in rock or tundra, including buildings and walls. They are found near most communities in the eastern Qikiqtani region.

DIET

Omnivore. Wheatears eat terrestrial insects and spiders, but also catch small snails and consume seeds and berries.

REPRODUCTION

The male establishes a breeding territory and the female selects a nest site within the territory, the cavity of which may be up to one metre deep. The female builds a small nest cup lined with dry vegetation and feathers of other birds, and there she lays five to eight pale blue eggs. The female incubates the eggs, and both parents feed and rear the chicks.

BEHAVIOUR

Wheatears are highly territorial and will drive other songbirds, even wheatears, away from their territory during breeding. Wheatears are generally solitary, but will form small flocks (up to 150 birds) during migration, although they rarely get close to one another on the ground. Their distinctive, undulating flight shows off their white rumps. While the female sits on the eggs, the male patrols the territory and gives out alarm calls if a threat is spotted.

PHOTO: JIM RICHARDS

RESEARCH AND MONITORING

Research on northern wheatears has been conducted around Iqaluit.

SURVIVAL AND STATUS

There is no estimate for the number of northern wheatears in Nunavut or North America. There are millions of them in northern Europe, but their numbers are declining. Weasels and foxes may depredate wheatear nests, and gulls, ravens, hawks, and falcons may eat the young and adult birds.

PHOTO: ROLF NAGEL

DID YOU KNOW?

The northern wheatear is probably the only songbird in North America that spends the winter in southern Africa, migrating across the Atlantic Ocean and back each year—a one-way journey of at least 7,500 kilometres. That's a long way to fly for a tiny bird! Scientists think that wheatears are a relatively recent addition to the Nunavut bird community—only since the last glaciation—and that they have not established a migration pattern within North America yet. Thus, they keep flying back and forth to Africa.

American Pipit

INUKTITUT NAME
Qainngaaq; qairngaaq; ingiiqtajuuq

FRENCH NAME
Pipit d'Amérique

SCIENTIFIC NAME
Anthus rubescens

PHOTO: ROLF NAGEL

APPEARANCE

Monomorphic. This small songbird weighs 18 to 26 grams and has a wingspan up to 28 centimetres. Both males and females have a drab, nondescript appearance. During the breeding season, the American pipit has light greyish and brown upperparts, with dark brown wings and tail. It has a distinctive, pale white or beige stripe through its eye, a creamy throat, and a creamy to light brown breast, belly, and undertail. Its breast and flanks are streaked with dark grey, and it has an obvious thin white bar on the feathers of its upper wing. Its bill is thin and black, and its legs and feet are black.

Breeding Only

RANGE

American pipits are found across all of Nunavut, except for the extreme southwest at the treeline, and the islands north of 74°N (although they were found at Truelove Lowlands on northern Devon Island). In the winter, they are found across the southern United States and throughout Mexico.

HABITAT

Pipits are common in dry Arctic and alpine tundra and meadows mixed with boulder fields, and are particularly common along streams and rivers. They occupy similar habitats in the winter.

DIET

Carnivore. Pipits feed on insects and spiders most of the year, as well as some mollusks and crustaceans. They occasionally consume seeds during migration and in the winter.

REPRODUCTION

Male pipits establish a territory, where the female chooses a protected nest site, often a hummock or location with vegetative concealment from above. She builds a nest from dead grasses and other vegetation, and then lays three to seven pale whitish eggs covered with reddish-brown spots, making them appear dark. The male brings food to the female during incubation, but not right to the nest. Instead he calls to her and she leaves the nest, takes the food, and then slips back onto the eggs. The female incubates the eggs, but both parents rear the chicks.

BEHAVIOUR

In contrast to other small birds like buntings and longspurs, pipits are inconspicuous, but they can be identified by the distinctive up-and-down bobbing of their tails. Female pipits on their nests are highly reluctant to leave, and usually only flush if a person stops within one metre of their nest and waits. Pipits form small flocks during migration and in the winter.

RESEARCH AND MONITORING

American pipits have been studied on Bylot and Baffin Islands.

SURVIVAL AND STATUS

Scientists do not know how many pipits there are in Nunavut or North America, but some surveys suggest that their population may be declining. Like other small ground-nesting birds, weasels and foxes may depredate pipit nests; gulls, ravens, hawks, and falcons may eat both young and adult birds.

? DID YOU KNOW?

Pipits are susceptible to mortality following severe weather, especially unexpected snowstorms during the breeding season.

PHOTO: JIM RICHARDS

Lapland Longspur

INUKTITUT NAME
Qirniqtaaq

FRENCH NAME
Bruant lapon

SCIENTIFIC NAME
Calcarius lapponicus

PHOTO: JIM RICHARDS

APPEARANCE

Dimorphic. This small songbird weighs 23 to 33 grams and has a wingspan of up to 29 centimetres. During the breeding season, the male has black and light brown streaked feathers on his back and tail, with light, rusty-red patches on his wing feathers. He has white underparts but black flanks under the wings. His tail is black but the outermost tail feathers are white. His head has a black crown and black feathers from the bill to behind the eye, including the chin, cheeks, throat, and breast. A thin white stripe separates the black feathers from the brownish feathers on his back and wings, and this stripe continues up the neck and cheek and joins on the forehead, making the black face look like a mask. His nape is a bright shade of rusty red, and there is often a yellow tinge to the white feathers between the nape and crown. The female has similar feathers on the back and nape, but lacks the black facial mask and breast. She has greyish-brown feathers on the cheeks, a striped crown, and black streaks on the white breast and flanks. The bill is yellow, while the legs and feet are black for both males and females.

■ Breeding Only

RANGE

Lapland longspurs are found across all of Nunavut except northwest Ellesmere Island and the islands in the northwest of Nunavut, including Amund Ringnes, Ellef Ringnes, and Axel Heiberg. In the winter, they are commonly found in open habitats of the central and southern United States.

HABITAT

Longspurs are common in wet tundra meadows and dry vegetated slopes, but they tend to avoid the rockier areas frequented by buntings. In the winter, they are common in any open areas that allow them to find seeds.

DIET

Omnivore. Longspurs eat a variety of seeds and insects in the summer, and primarily eat seeds in the winter.

REPRODUCTION

The male longspur establishes a territory, and there the female chooses a protected nest site, often a hummock or location with concealment from above. She builds her nest from dead grasses, lines it with found feathers or fur, and then lays one to eight pale greenish-white eggs heavily blotched with light brown speckles. The female incubates the eggs, but both parents rear the chicks.

BEHAVIOUR

Lapland longspurs are highly gregarious, often nesting in high densities, and can form massive flocks in the winter, numbering in the millions of birds. During the breeding season, bright male longspurs are conspicuous, as they perch on rocks and sing.

RESEARCH AND MONITORING

Lapland longspurs have been studied on the Melville Peninsula, and on Devon, Baffin, Bylot, Southampton, Bathurst, and Prince of Wales islands.

SURVIVAL AND STATUS

Scientists estimate that there may be 40 million longspurs breeding in the North American Arctic, a large proportion of which come from Nunavut. There is no consistent pattern of overall population trends for this species. In some areas, the population has declined, and in others, the population has remained stable over time. Weasels and foxes may depredate longspur nests, and gulls, ravens, hawks, and falcons may eat both the young and adult birds.

 DID YOU KNOW?

Lapland longspurs are probably the most abundant Arctic-nesting terrestrial bird worldwide, and are the most abundant bird in Nunavut!

PHOTO: ROLF NAGEL

FAMILY EMBERIZIDAE

Savannah Sparrow

INUKTITUT NAME
Nunamiutaq qupanuarjuk

FRENCH NAME
Bruant des prés

SCIENTIFIC NAME
Passerculus sandwichensis

APPEARANCE

Monomorphic. This small songbird weighs 15 to 30 grams and has an average wingspan of just 17 centimetres. The males are slightly larger than the females. During the breeding season, this sparrow's nape, back, wings, and rump are greyish brown and streaked with darker chocolate centres and lighter tan edges. The outer wing and tail feathers are brown. The throat, breast, flanks, and belly are whitish to pale beige, streaked with brown on the breast and flanks. On the head, the crown usually has a tan or white stripe surrounded by streaky brown, and another stripe of yellow from the bill to above and behind the eye (like an eyebrow). A whitish strip often extends back from the lower bill, and borders a brown cheek patch under the eye. The bill is dark brown on top and pink below, and the legs and feet are pinkish.

Breeding Only

RANGE

Savannah sparrows are found across the Kivalliq region south of Rankin Inlet, from Rankin northwest to the Adelaide Peninsula, and throughout the western mainland Kitikmeot region. Some savannah sparrows live on the southern part of Victoria Island. A few birds make it as far north as 76°N on Devon Island. In the winter they are common in the southern United States and Mexico.

HABITAT

Savannah sparrows are common in open, vegetated tundra meadows. In the winter, they are common in any open areas that allow them to find seeds.

DIET

Omnivore. Savannah sparrows eat a variety of seeds, berries, and insects throughout the year.

REPRODUCTION

The male savannah sparrow establishes a territory, and the female chooses a protected nest site, often with overhanging vegetation concealing the nest from above. She builds the nest from dead grasses, lines it with fine, interwoven vegetation, and then lays two to six pale greenish eggs with brown speckles and streaks. The female incubates the eggs, and both parents rear the chicks.

BEHAVIOUR

Savannah sparrows are territorial during breeding but are gregarious during migration and in the winter. Some birds of this species are polygynous, so a male may have more than one mate in his territory.

RESEARCH AND MONITORING

Savannah sparrows have been studied near Kugluktuk.

SURVIVAL AND STATUS

Population size and trends are unknown for savannah sparrows, although significant population shifts in different parts of the range suggest a cycle of abundance. Weasels and foxes depredate sparrow nests, and gulls, ravens, hawks, and falcons eat the young and adult birds.

?

DID YOU KNOW?

The savannah sparrow has 17 recognized subspecies, making it one of the most variable species in North America.

PHOTO: JIM RICHARDS

FAMILY EMBERIZIDAE

Snow Bunting

INUKTITUT NAME
Qaquqtaaq; qaulluqtaaq

FRENCH NAME
Bruant des neiges

SCIENTIFIC NAME
Plectrophenax nivalis

PHOTO: JIM RICHARDS

APPEARANCE

Dimorphic. This small songbird weighs 30 to 40 grams and has a wingspan of approximately 35 centimetres. During the breeding season, the males are entirely black and white. They have white heads, napes, breasts, bellies, rumps, and outer tail feathers. Their backs and central tail feathers are black, and their wings have black outer and white inner feathers. Females also have black-and-white wings during breeding, but they have reddish-brown feathers streaked with grey on their backs, and the feathers on their crowns, as well as those extending from their bills to above their eyes, are pale reddish brown. Their undersides are white with a pale hint of reddish brown on the sides. In both sexes, the legs and feet are black. The male has a black bill during breeding, while the female has a brownish one.

■ Breeding

RANGE

Snow buntings are found all across Nunavut, and some may occasionally overwinter in the territory, although most migrate to open areas of southern Canada and the northern United States.

HABITAT

Snow buntings prefer rocky areas in vegetated tundra, as they require rock crevices or cavities for nesting. They may nest in cracks on cliffs at altitude, and may also nest in buildings and piled materials near human settlements. In the winter, they are commonly found in open, grassy fields.

DIET

Omnivore. Buntings eat seeds, buds, and grasses, but also consume insects, spiders, crustaceans, and mollusks found along the shoreline.

REPRODUCTION

The male bunting establishes a territory, both sexes investigate nest sites in cavities there, and then the female builds a nest from vegetation. She lines her nest with feathers she gathers, and in it she lays two to eight pale blue eggs speckled with light brown. Females nesting farther north lay more eggs. The female incubates the eggs, and both parents rear the chicks.

BEHAVIOUR

Snow buntings nest in cavities, so there may be high competition for nest sites. For this reason, the male bunting arrives weeks before the female to secure a territory and breeding site. Unlike many other Arctic songbirds, the male bunting feeds his mates while she is on her nest. This occurs because the female is trying to keep her eggs warm in a cold cavity. During migration and in the winter, buntings are gregarious and may occur in large flocks.

PHOTO: MARK MALLORY

RESEARCH AND MONITORING

Snow buntings have been studied on the Melville Peninsula, in Iqaluit, on Jenny Lind Island, at Cape Vera and Truelove Lowlands on Devon Island, and in the East Bay Migratory Bird Sanctuary.

SURVIVAL AND STATUS

There may be as many as 8 million snow buntings in North America, a large proportion of which come from Nunavut. Recent data suggest that the snow bunting population may be in serious decline, but the reasons for this are unknown. Bunting nests may be depredated by weasels and foxes, and young and adult birds may be eaten by gulls, ravens, hawks, and falcons.

PHOTO: ROLP NAGEL

LOCAL ECOLOGICAL KNOWLEDGE

The arrival of snow buntings is a sign that spring is coming in the Arctic. Young boys practice their hunting skills by trying to hit buntings with rocks.

? DID YOU KNOW?

Snow buntings are one of three bird species that have been observed close to the North Pole.

White-crowned Sparrow

INUKTITUT NAME
Qupanuarjuk niaqua taqsalik

FRENCH NAME
Bruant à couronne blanche

SCIENTIFIC NAME
Zonotrichia leucophrys (subspecies *leucophrys, gambelii, pugetensis, nuttalli*)

PHOTO: JIM RICHARDS

APPEARANCE

Monomorphic. This small songbird weighs 20 to 35 grams and has a wingspan of up to 26 centimetres. During the breeding season, this sparrow's back and wings are light grey streaked with rich brown, black, and white. Its wings have two distinctive white wing bars, visible in flight or when the wings are folded. Its tail is long, and both its tail and rump are greyish brown. Its distinctive feature is the top of the head, which has two black stripes separated by a broad white stripe through the crown. Another white stripe lies above each eye, and a black stripe extends backwards from the eye to the back of the nape. Collectively this creates seven stripes, alternating black then white, from eye to eye. The rest of the cheeks, chin, throat, and breast are grey, fading to pale grey-brown on the belly. The bill is orange and the legs and feet are pink.

RANGE

The white-crowned sparrow is found on the mainland of central and western Nunavut, although a few have been found on Victoria, Somerset, Bathurst, and Baffin Islands. It does not occur in the northeast Kivalliq region, nor is it found near the Melville or Boothia Peninsulas. It winters throughout the United States and northern Mexico.

Breeding Only

HABITAT

This sparrow inhabits a wide range of habitats, including open, vegetated tundra through to the edge of the treeline. The species requires bare ground for foraging and patchy, dense vegetation for nesting. In the winter, they are common on farmland, and in urban and forested habitats.

DIET

Omnivore. White-crowned sparrows eat seeds, grass, fruit, and insects all through the year.

REPRODUCTION

The male sparrow establishes a territory, and the female chooses a protected nest site, usually among dense, concealing vegetation. She builds the nest from dead grasses, lines it with fine vegetation, and then lays three to seven pale, greenish-white eggs heavily blotched with reddish brown (clutches are larger for birds nesting farther north). The female incubates the eggs, and both parents rear the chicks.

BEHAVIOUR

Sparrows are territorial during the breeding season, but they often form mixed-species feeding flocks in the winter.

SURVIVAL AND STATUS

There is no good estimate of the population size of this sparrow species, and counts during the winter suggest populations are declining in some regions and increasing in others, so an overall trend for North America is unclear.

DID YOU KNOW?

The white-crowned sparrow is one of the best-studied songbirds in North America, yet no research has been conducted in Nunavut.

FAMILY FRINGILLIDAE
Hoary Redpoll

INUKTITUT NAME
Saksagiaq

FRENCH NAME
Sizerin blanchatre

SCIENTIFIC NAME
Acanthis hornemanni

PHOTO: GERALD ROMANCHUK

APPEARANCE

Dimorphic. This tiny songbird weighs 11 to 20 grams and has a wingspan of about 23 centimetres. It often appears to have puffy, loose plumage. During the breeding season, the male has a distinctive red or dark pink forehead and a black chin. The head is pale brown streaked with darker brown, and the back is streaky, dark brown. The rump is white while the upper tail is dark. The underparts are white, although there is a pinkish hue to the breast. The female is similar overall to the male, except that she lacks red everywhere but the forehead, and the breast is lightly streaked with brown, giving her a slightly darker appearance than the male. Redpolls have stubby yellow bills and black legs and feet.

Breeding Only

RANGE

Hoary redpolls may be found across all of mainland Nunavut—on Southampton, North Baffin, Devon, Bathurst, Ellesmere, and Axel Heiberg Islands. They spend the winter throughout the open habitats of Canada, and as far north as the southern part of Baffin Island.

HABITAT

Redpolls are common on rocky slopes and areas of dry heath vegetation in warm, dry interior areas where microclimates allow shrubs to grow. They may live at elevations of up to 400 metres. In the winter, they can be found in open woodlands and along field edges.

DIET

Herbivore. Hoary redpolls eat seeds, buds, and the fruiting parts of plants. They may consume insects during breeding, although this has received little study.

REPRODUCTION

Pairs may reuse old nests. The male redpoll chooses a breeding area and the female constructs a nest in low vegetation (often in a willow) or in rocky crevices. She uses grasses to build the nest, lines it with feathers and soft material, and in it lays one to six bluish eggs covered in reddish-brown speckles. The female incubates, and the male brings her food during incubation. Both parents feed and rear the chicks.

BEHAVIOUR

Redpolls are very gregarious, nesting in loose associations and travelling in flocks of up to 50 birds in the winter. Redpolls have storage compartments in their throats where they keep seeds, which they can regurgitate, shell, and eat later. This allows them to get enough energy to survive the cold Arctic winter nights. When food is located, redpolls may spend up to 22 hours engaged in non-stop feeding.

RESEARCH AND MONITORING

There has been very little research on redpolls in Nunavut, other than observations from expeditions, and some diet studies on Bathurst Island.

SURVIVAL AND STATUS

There is no estimate of the population size of hoary redpolls in Nunavut or in North America, but recent surveys suggest that their population is in decline.

? DID YOU KNOW?
Redpolls are the smallest birds in Nunavut.

PHOTO: RAY WILSON

FAMILY PHASIANIDAE

Rock Ptarmigan

INUKTITUT NAME
Aqiggiq atajulik

FRENCH NAME
Lagopède alpin

SCIENTIFIC NAME
Lagopus mutus

APPEARANCE

Monomorphic. This medium-sized bird resembles a chicken, weighs 440 to 660 grams, and has a wingspan of 60 centimetres. In the winter, the ptarmigan is all white except for a black tail and a small black streak through the eye, which is a distinguishing feature of this species. In the summer, the female is highly cryptic, with mottled, brownish-black feathers that have light tan streaks and fringes, giving the appearance of "salt-and-pepper" barring. Male feathers are similar, except that males tend to be more brownish grey, and have finer markings. The male has distinctive, orange-red, fleshy combs that stand up above his eye; the female also has a comb, but it is smaller and paler orange. All ptarmigan have feathered legs and feet, which work like snowshoes on the snow.

Resident year-round

RANGE

Rock ptarmigan are one of the very few year-round avian residents of Nunavut. They may be found anywhere in the territory north of 62°N. High Arctic birds migrate to more southern tundra during the winter.

HABITAT

Rock ptarmigan are common in dry, barren alpine tundra with rocky outcrops. In the winter, they may move to areas that support some shrubby vegetation with buds.

DIET

Omnivore. Ptarmigan principally eat the leaves, flowers, seeds, and buds of trees and shrubs, but they may also eat insects in the summer.

REPRODUCTION

The male rock ptarmigan may make several scrapes, but the female scrapes the nest she will use, usually in a dry, protected area near a rock or outcrop. She lines it with vegetation and sometimes

156 | Common Birds of Nunavut

feathers, and lays eight to ten eggs that are initially red, but smear or rub down to a pale pinkish brown with dark brown splotches. The female incubates the eggs and rears the young.

BEHAVIOUR

Rock ptarmigan are the quintessential Arctic bird, staying in tundra regions year-round. They are tame and can be approached quite closely before they flush or run away. Males are strongly territorial during the breeding season, but both sexes are gregarious and may form large flocks during the winter. After breeding, males rub themselves in the dirt to make their white feathers less conspicuous to predators, before they moult into their camouflage pattern. Rock ptarmigan burrow into snowdrifts during very cold weather and can remain there most of the day.

PHOTO: MARK MALLORY

RESEARCH AND MONITORING

Research on ptarmigan has been undertaken in the Kivalliq region near the Melville Peninsula, and in the Kitikmeot region near the Kent Peninsula.

SURVIVAL AND STATUS

There is no reliable estimate for the number of rock ptarmigan in Nunavut. The North American population could be anywhere between 2 and 8 million birds, many of which would occur in Nunavut. Numbers of birds follow a ten-year cycle in abundance, but there are no data on long-term trends. Hunters in Nunavut harvest at least 13,000 ptarmigan annually. Ptarmigan are key prey for falcons, but adults, eggs, or young may also be eaten by gulls, ravens, hawks, jaegers, weasels, foxes, and wolves.

LOCAL ECOLOGICAL KNOWLEDGE

Traditionally, ptarmigan skins were used to clean pots. As well, the stomach of the bird was removed, inflated, and tied off at each end to be used as a rattle or decoration. In some communities, Inuit women have races to see who can skin a ptarmigan the fastest!

DID YOU KNOW?

The rock ptarmigan is the territorial bird of Nunavut, and comes from the Gaelic word *tarmachan*, meaning mountaineer.

PHOTO: JIM RICHARDS

FAMILY PHASIANIDAE
Willow Ptarmigan

INUKTITUT NAME
Aqiggiq; aqiggivik

FRENCH NAME
Lagopède des saules

SCIENTIFIC NAME
Lagopus lagopus

APPEARANCE

Monomorphic. This medium-sized bird resembles a chicken, weighs 430 to 810 grams, and has a wingspan of up to 61 centimetres. In the winter, the bird is all white except for its black eyes and tail feathers (which are largely hidden). In the summer, the female is highly cryptic, with mottled brownish feathers that are more reddish than those of the rock ptarmigan and white wings. Male feathers are similar, except that males tend to be more reddish, particularly in the head and neck. Their bellies and underparts remain white. The male has distinctive, orange-red, fleshy combs that stand up above his eye; the female also has a comb, but it is smaller and paler orange. All ptarmigan have feathered legs and feet, which work like snowshoes on the snow.

Resident year-round

RANGE

Many willow ptarmigan are year-round avian residents of Nunavut. They are found anywhere in Nunavut south of 74°N, and only along the western part of Baffin Island, giving them a more southerly and westerly distribution than that of rock ptarmigan. Birds nesting farther north migrate to more southern tundra during the winter.

HABITAT

Willow ptarmigan are common in marshy coastal tundra and around ponds—generally in habitats with more lush vegetation than those preferred by rock ptarmigan.

DIET

Omnivore. Willow ptarmigan principally eat the leaves, flowers, seeds, and buds of trees and shrubs, but they may also eat insects in the summer.

REPRODUCTION

Most willow ptarmigan have only one mate, but in some cases a male will be partnered with more than one female. The female constructs the nest, usually in vegetation with overhead concealment, which she lines with dry grass, leaves, and feathers, and then she lays four to eleven cream-coloured eggs with dark brown splotches. Only the female incubates the eggs, but unlike other ptarmigan, the male remains with the female to help rear the young.

BEHAVIOUR

Willow ptarmigan can be very tame and thus can be approached closely before they flush or run away. Males are strongly territorial during the breeding season, but birds are gregarious and may form flocks of up to 2,000 birds during the winter. Like shorebirds, willow ptarmigan will perform distraction displays to lure predators away from their nests or their chicks.

PHOTO: JIM RICHARDS

SURVIVAL AND STATUS

There is no reliable estimate for the number of willow ptarmigan in Nunavut. Numbers of birds follow an eight- to eleven-year cycle in abundance, but there are no statistics on long-term trends. Hunters in Nunavut harvest at least 13,000 ptarmigan annually. Ptarmigan are key prey for falcons, but adults, eggs, or young may also be eaten by gulls, ravens, hawks, jaegers, weasels, foxes, and wolves.

LOCAL ECOLOGICAL KNOWLEDGE

Traditionally, ptarmigan skins were used to clean pots. As well, the stomach of the bird was removed, inflated, and tied off at each end to be used as a rattle or decoration.

DID YOU KNOW?

Ptarmigan are masters of camouflage. They usually sit motionless on their nests when predators approach, relying on their cryptic feathers to hide them. Arctic foxes have been seen walking within two metres of ptarmigan nests and moving on, not seeing the birds.

What Birds Are Found in Nunavut?

There are 268 species of birds that have been observed in Nunavut. The table below lists all of these species, their scientific names, where they have been observed, and whether they are known to breed in Nunavut (Richards and White, 2008). A question mark means that breeding is suggested or suspected but has not been confirmed.

Species	Scientific name	Where is it found?		Breeds in Nunavut?
		Mainland	Islands	
Loons				
Red-throated loon	Gavia stellata	Y	Y	Y
Pacific loon	Gavia pacifica	Y	Y	Y
Common loon	Gavia immer	Y	Y	Y
Yellow-billed loon	Gavia adamsii	Y	Y	Y
Grebes				
Pied-billed grebe	Podilymbus podiceps	N	Y	N
Horned grebe	Podiceps auritus	Y	Y	Y
Red-necked grebe	Podiceps grisegena	N	Y	N
Petrels				
Northern fulmar	Fulmarus glacialis	Y	Y	Y
Greater shearwater	Puffinus gravis	N	Y	N
Sooty shearwater	Puffinus griseus	N	Y	N
Short-tailed shearwater	Puffinus tenuirostris	Y	N	N
Wilson's storm-petrel	Oceanites oceanicus	N	Y	N
Leach's storm-petrel	Oceanodroma leucorhoa	N	Y	N
Gannets, pelicans, and cormorants				
Northern gannet	Morus bassanus	N	Y	N
American white pelican	Pelecanus erythrorhynchos	Y	Y	Y
Double-crested cormorant	Phalacrocorax auritus	N	Y	Y
Herons and bitterns				
American bittern	Botaurus lentiginosus	Y	Y	Y
Great blue heron	Ardea herodias	Y	Y	N
Cattle egret	Bubulcus ibis	Y	N	N
Ducks, geese, and swans				
Tundra swan	Cygnus columbianus	Y	Y	Y
Trumpeter swan	Cygnus buccinator	Y	Y	?
Greater white-fronted goose	Anser albifrons	Y	Y	Y
Snow goose	Chen caerulescens	Y	Y	Y

Species	Scientific name	Where is it found?		Breeds in Nunavut?
		Mainland	Islands	
Ross's goose	*Chen rossi*	Y	Y	Y
Brant	*Branta bernicla*	Y	Y	Y
Barnacle goose	*Branta leucopsis*	N	Y	N
Cackling goose	*Branta hutchinsii*	Y	Y	Y
Canada goose	*Branta canadensis*	Y	Y	Y
Wood duck	*Aix sponsa*	N	Y	N
Gadwall	*Anas strepera*	N	Y	N
American wigeon	*Anas americana*	Y	Y	Y
American black duck	*Anas rubripes*	Y	Y	Y
Mallard	*Anas platyrhynchos*	Y	Y	Y
Blue-winged teal	*Anas discors*	N	Y	?
Northern shoveler	*Anas clypeata*	Y	Y	?
Northern pintail	*Anas acuta*	Y	Y	Y
Green-winged teal	*Anas crecca*	Y	Y	Y
Canvasback	*Aythya valisineria*	N	Y	N
Redhead	*Aythya americana*	N	Y	N
Ring-necked duck	*Aythya collaris*	N	Y	?
Greater scaup	*Aythya marila*	Y	Y	Y
Lesser scaup	*Aythya affinis*	Y	Y	Y
Steller's eider	*Polysticta stelleri*	N	Y	N
King eider	*Somateria spectabilis*	Y	Y	Y
Common eider	*Somateria mollissima*	Y	Y	Y
Harlequin duck	*Histrionicus histrionicus*	Y	Y	Y
Surf scoter	*Melanitta perspicillata*	Y	Y	Y
White-winged scoter	*Melanitta fusca*	Y	Y	Y
Black scoter	*Melanitta nigra*	Y	Y	Y
Long-tailed duck	*Clangula hyemalis*	Y	Y	Y
Bufflehead	*Bucephala albeola*	Y	N	?
Common goldeneye	*Bucephala clangula*	Y	Y	Y
Barrow's goldeneye	*Bucephala islandica*	N	Y	N
Hooded merganser	*Lophodytes cucullatus*	Y	Y	Y
Common merganser	*Mergus merganser*	Y	Y	Y
Red-breasted merganser	*Mergus serrator*	Y	Y	Y
Vultures, hawks, eagles, and falcons				
Turkey vulture	*Cathartes aura*	Y	Y	N
Osprey	*Pandion haliaetus*	Y	Y	Y

Species	Scientific name	Where is it found?		Breeds in Nunavut?
		Mainland	Islands	
Bald eagle	*Haliaeetus leucocephalus*	Y	Y	Y
Northern harrier	*Circus cyaneus*	Y	Y	?
Sharp-shinned hawk	*Accipter striatus*	Y	Y	?
Northern goshawk	*Accipter gentilis*	Y	Y	?
Swainson's hawk	*Buteo swainsoni*	Y	N	N
Red-tailed hawk	*Buteo jamaicensis*	N	Y	?
Rough-legged hawk	*Buteo lagopus*	Y	Y	Y
Golden eagle	*Aquila chrysaetos*	Y	Y	Y
American kestrel	*Falco sparverius*	Y	Y	Y
Merlin	*Falco columbarius*	Y	Y	Y
Gyrfalcon	*Falco rusticolus*	Y	Y	Y
Peregrine falcon	*Falco peregrinus*	Y	Y	Y
Ptarmigan and grouse				
Spruce grouse	*Falcipennis canadensis*	Y	Y	Y
Willow ptarmigan	*Lagopus lagopus*	Y	Y	Y
Rock ptarmigan	*Lagopus muta*	Y	Y	Y
White-tailed ptarmigan	*Lagopus leucura*	Y	N	N
Sharp-tailed grouse	*Tympanuchus phasianellus*	N	Y	Y
Cranes, rails, and coots				
Yellow rail	*Coturnicops noveboracensis*	N	Y	?
Corn crake	*Crex crex*	N	Y	N
American coot	*Fulica americana*	Y	Y	N
Sandhill crane	*Grus canadensis*	Y	Y	Y
Whooping crane	*Grus americana*	Y	Y	N
Shorebirds				
Northern lapwing	*Vanellus vanellus*	N	Y	N
Black-bellied plover	*Pluvialis squatarola*	Y	Y	Y
American golden-plover	*Pluvialis dominica*	Y	Y	Y
Common ringed plover	*Charadrius hiaticula*	N	Y	Y
Semipalmated Plover	*Charadrius semipalmatus*	Y	Y	Y
Piping plover	*Charadrius melodus*	N	Y	N
Killdeer	*Charadrius vociferus*	Y	Y	Y
American avocet	*Recurvirostra americana*	N	Y	N
Spotted sandpiper	*Actitis macularius*	Y	Y	Y
Solitary sandpiper	*Tringa solitaria*	Y	Y	?
Greater yellowlegs	*Tringa melanoleuca*	Y	Y	?

Species	Scientific name	Where is it found?		Breeds in Nunavut?
		Mainland	Islands	
Lesser yellowlegs	*Tringa flavipes*	Y	Y	Y
Upland sandpiper	*Bartramia longicauda*	Y	N	N
Eskimo curlew (extinct?)	*Numenius borealis*	(Y)	(Y)	(?)
Whimbrel	*Numenius phaeopus*	Y	Y	Y
Long-billed curlew	*Numenius americanus*	N	Y	N
Hudsonian godwit	*Limosa haemastica*	Y	Y	?
Marbled godwit	*Limosa fedoa*	N	Y	Y
Ruddy turnstone	*Arenaria interpres*	Y	Y	Y
Red knot	*Calidris cornutus*	Y	Y	Y
Sanderling	*Calidris alba*	Y	Y	Y
Semipalmated sandpiper	*Calidris pusilla*	Y	Y	Y
Least sandpiper	*Calidris minutilla*	Y	Y	Y
White-rumped sandpiper	*Calidris fuscicollis*	Y	Y	Y
Baird's sandpiper	*Calidris bairdii*	Y	Y	Y
Pectoral sandpiper	*Calidris melanotos*	Y	Y	Y
Purple sandpiper	*Calidris maritima*	Y	Y	Y
Dunlin	*Calidris alpina*	Y	Y	Y
Stilt sandpiper	*Calidris himantopus*	Y	Y	Y
Buff-breasted sandpiper	*Tryngites subruficollis*	Y	Y	Y
Ruff	*Philomachus pugnax*	N	Y	N
Short-billed dowitcher	*Limnodromus griseus*	Y	Y	Y
Wilson's snipe	*Gallinago delicata*	Y	Y	Y
Wilson's phalarope	*Phalaropus tricolor*	N	Y	N
Red-necked phalarope	*Phalaropus lobatus*	Y	Y	Y
Red phalarope	*Phalaropus fulicarius*	Y	Y	Y
Gulls, terns, and jaegers				
Pomarine jaeger	*Stercorarius pomarinus*	Y	Y	Y
Parasitic jaeger	*Stercorarius parasiticus*	Y	Y	Y
Long-tailed jaeger	*Stercorarius longicauda*	Y	Y	Y
Black-legged kittiwake	*Rissa tridactyla*	Y	Y	Y
Ivory gull	*Pagophila eburnea*	Y	Y	Y
Sabine's gull	*Xema sabini*	Y	Y	Y
Bonaparte's gull	*Chroicocephalus philadelphia*	Y	Y	Y
Black-headed gull	*Chroicocephalus ridibundus*	N	Y	N
Little gull	*Hydrocoloeus minutus*	N	Y	?
Ross's gull	*Rhodostethia rosea*	Y	Y	Y

Species	Scientific name	Where is it found?		Breeds in Nunavut?
		Mainland	Islands	
Franklin's gull	*Leucophaeus pipixcan*	N	Y	N
Mew gull	*Larus canus*	Y	Y	Y
Ring-billed gull	*Larus delawarensis*	Y	Y	Y
California gull	*Larus californicus*	Y	Y	N
Herring gull	*Larus argentatus*	Y	Y	Y
Thayer's gull	*Larus thayeri*	Y	Y	Y
Iceland gull	*Larus glaucoides*	Y	Y	Y
Lesser black-backed gull	*Larus fuscus*	Y	Y	N
Slaty-backed gull	*Larus schistisagus*	N	Y	N
Glaucous-winged gull	*Larus glaucescens*	N	Y	N
Glaucous gull	*Larus hyperboreus*	Y	Y	Y
Great black-backed gull	*Larus marinus*	Y	Y	Y
Caspian tern	*Hydroprogne caspia*	N	Y	Y
Black tern	*Chlidonias niger*	N	Y	Y
Common tern	*Sterna hirundo*	Y	Y	Y
Arctic tern	*Sterna paradisaea*	Y	Y	Y
Auks				
Dovekie	*Alle alle*	Y	Y	Y
Common murre	*Uria aalge*	N	Y	N
Thick-billed murre	*Uria lomvia*	Y	Y	Y
Razorbill	*Alca torda*	N	Y	Y
Black guillemot	*Cepphus grylle*	Y	Y	Y
Atlantic puffin	*Fratercula arctica*	N	Y	Y
Horned puffin	*Fratercula corniculata*	Y	N	N
Tufted puffin	*Fratercula cirrhata*	Y	N	N
Doves				
Mourning dove	*Zenaida macroura*	N	Y	N
Passenger pigeon (extinct)	*Ectopistes migratorius*	N	(Y)	N
Owls				
Great horned owl	*Bubo virginianus*	Y	Y	?
Snowy owl	*Bubo scandiaca*	Y	Y	Y
Northern hawk owl	*Surnia ulula*	Y	Y	?
Long-eared owl	*Asio otus*	N	Y	N
Short-eared owl	*Asio flammeus*	Y	Y	Y
Swifts and goatsuckers				
Common nighthawk	*Chordeiles minor*	Y	Y	?

Species	Scientific name	Where is it found?		Breeds in Nunavut?
		Mainland	Islands	
Black swift	*Cypseloides niger*	N	Y	N
Chimney swift	*Chaetura pelagica*	N	Y	N
Kingfishers				
Belted kingfisher	*Megaceryle alcyon*	Y	Y	?
Woodpeckers				
Yellow-bellied sapsucker	*Sphyrapicus varius*	N	Y	?
Downy woodpecker	*Picoides pubescens*	N	Y	N
Hairy woodpecker	*Picoides villosus*	Y	Y	Y
American three-toed woodpecker	*Picoides dorsalis*	Y	Y	?
Black-blacked woodpecker	*Picoides arcticus*	N	Y	?
Northern flicker	*Colaptes auratus*	Y	Y	Y
Flycatchers				
Olive-sided flycatcher	*Contopus cooperi*	N	Y	N
Yellow-bellied flycatcher	*Empidonax flaviventris*	N	Y	N
Alder flycatcher	*Empidonax alnorum*	N	Y	?
Eastern phoebe	*Sayornis phoebe*	Y	N	N
Say's phoebe	*Sayornis saya*	Y	Y	N
Great crested flycatcher	*Myiarchus crinitus*	Y	N	N
Western kingbird	*Tyrannus verticalis*	Y	Y	N
Eastern kingbird	*Tyrannus tyrannus*	Y	Y	N
Fork-tailed flycatcher	*Tyrannus savana*	N	Y	N
Shrikes and vireos				
Northern shrike	*Lanius excubitor*	Y	Y	Y
Philadelphia vireo	*Vireo philadelphicus*	N	Y	N
Red-eyed vireo	*Vireo olivaceus*	Y	Y	?
Jays				
Grey jay	*Perisoreus canadensis*	Y	Y	Y
Black-billed magpie	*Pica hudsonia*	Y	N	N
American crow	*Corvus brachyrhynchos*	Y	Y	?
Common raven	*Corvus corax*	Y	Y	Y
Swallows				
Purple martin	*Progne subis*	N	Y	N
Tree swallow	*Tachycineta bicolor*	Y	Y	?
Violet-green swallow	*Tachycineta thalassina*	N	Y	N
Bank swallow	*Riparia riparia*	N	Y	N

Species	Scientific name	Where is it found?		Breeds in Nunavut?
		Mainland	Islands	
Cliff swallow	*Petrochelidon pyrrhonota*	Y	Y	Y
Barn swallow	*Hirundo rustica*	Y	Y	Y
Chickadees, nuthatches, creepers, and wrens				
Boreal chickadee	*Poecile hudsonica*	Y	Y	Y
Red-breasted nuthatch	*Sitta canadensis*	N	Y	?
Brown creeper	*Certhia americana*	N	Y	N
Winter wren	*Troglodytes troglodytes*	N	Y	?
Kinglets				
Golden-crowned kinglet	*Regulus satrapa*	N	Y	?
Ruby-crowned kinglet	*Regulus calendula*	Y	Y	Y
Larks and thrushes				
Horned lark	*Eremophila alpestris*	Y	Y	Y
Northern wheatear	*Oenanthe oenanthe*	Y	Y	Y
Mountain bluebird	*Sialia currucoides*	Y	Y	?
Grey-cheeked thrush	*Catharus minimus*	Y	Y	Y
Swainson's thrush	*Catharus ustulatus*	Y	Y	?
Hermit thrush	*Catharus guttatus*	Y	Y	?
Fieldfare	*Turdus pilaris*	N	Y	N
American robin	*Turdus migratorius*	Y	Y	Y
Varied thrush	*Ixoreus naevius*	N	Y	N
Mockingbirds				
Grey catbird	*Dumetella carolinensis*	N	Y	?
Northern mockingbird	*Mimus polyglottos*	Y	Y	N
Brown thrasher	*Toxostoma rufum*	Y	Y	N
Starlings				
European starling	*Sturnus vulgaris*	Y	Y	Y
Wagtails and pipits				
Eastern yellow wagtail	*Motacilla tschutschensis*	N	Y	N
American pipit	*Anthus rubescens*	Y	Y	Y
Waxwings				
Bohemian waxwing	*Bombycilla garrulous*	Y	Y	N
Cedar waxwing	*Bombycilla cedrorum*	N	Y	?
Wood warblers				
Tennessee warbler	*Vermivora peregrine*	Y	Y	?
Orange-crowned warbler	*Vermivora celata*	Y	Y	?
Yellow warbler	*Dendroica petechia*	Y	Y	Y

Species	Scientific name	Where is it found?		Breeds in Nunavut?
		Mainland	Islands	
Magnolia warbler	*Dendroica magnolia*	N	Y	?
Cape May warbler	*Dendroica tigrina*	N	Y	Y
Black-throated blue warbler	*Dendroica caerulescens*	N	Y	N
Yellow-rumped warbler	*Dendroica coronata*	Y	Y	Y
Black-throated green warbler	*Dendroica virens*	N	Y	N
Blackburnian warbler	*Dendroica fusca*	Y	N	N
Palm warbler	*Dendroica palmarum*	Y	Y	?
Bay-breasted warbler	*Dendroica castanea*	N	Y	N
Blackpoll warbler	*Dendroica striata*	Y	Y	?
Black-and-white warbler	*Mniotilta varia*	N	Y	N
American redstart	*Setophala ruticilla*	Y	Y	N
Northern waterthrush	*Seiurus noveboracensis*	Y	Y	?
Common yellowthroat	*Geothlypis trichas*	N	Y	?
Hooded warbler	*Wilsonia citrina*	N	Y	N
Wilson's warbler	*Wilsonia pusilla*	Y	Y	Y
Tanagers and grosbeaks				
Western tanager	*Piranga ludoviciana*	N	Y	N
Rose-breasted grosbeak	*Pheuticus ludovicianus*	Y	N	N
Sparrows				
Spotted towhee	*Pipilo maculatus*	Y	N	N
American tree sparrow	*Spizella arborea*	Y	Y	Y
Chipping sparrow	*Spizella passerina*	Y	Y	N
Clay-coloured sparrow	*Spizella pallida*	Y	N	N
Savannah sparrow	*Passerculus sandwichensis*	Y	Y	Y
Le Conte's sparrow	*Ammodramus leconteii*	N	Y	?
Nelson's sparrow	*Ammodramus nelsoni*	N	Y	?
Fox sparrow	*Passerella iliaca*	Y	Y	Y
Song sparrow	*Melospiza melodia*	Y	Y	?
Lincoln's sparrow	*Melospiza lincolnii*	Y	Y	Y
Swamp sparrow	*Melospiza georgiana*	N	Y	Y
White-throated sparrow	*Zonotrichia albicollis*	Y	Y	Y
Harris's sparrow	*Zonotrichia querula*	Y	Y	Y
White-crowned sparrow	*Zonotrichia leucophrys*	Y	Y	Y
Dark-eyed junco	*Junco hyemalis*	Y	Y	Y
Lapland longspur	*Calcarius lapponicus*	Y	Y	Y
Smith's longspur	*Calcarius pictus*	Y	Y	Y

Species	Scientific name	Where is it found?		Breeds in Nunavut?
		Mainland	Islands	
Snow bunting	*Plectrophenax nivalis*	Y	Y	Y
Blackbirds				
Bobolink	*Dolichonyx oryzivorus*	N	Y	N
Red-winged blackbird	*Agelaius phoeniceus*	N	Y	?
Western meadowlark	*Sturnella neglecta*	N	Y	N
Yellow-headed blackbird	*Xanthocephalus xanthocephalus*	Y	Y	N
Rusty blackbird	*Euphagus carolinus*	Y	Y	Y
Brewer's blackbird	*Euphagus cyanocephalus*	Y	N	N
Common grackle	*Quiscalus quiscula*	Y	Y	N
Brown-headed cowbird	*Molothrus ater*	Y	Y	?
Baltimore oriole	*Icterus galbula*	Y	N	N
Finches				
Grey-crowned Rosy-finch	*Leucosticte tephrocotis*	Y	N	N
Pine grosbeak	*Pinicola enucleator*	Y	Y	?
Purple finch	*Carpodacus purpureus*	Y	Y	?
White-winged crossbill	*Loxia leucoptera*	Y	Y	?
Common redpoll	*Carduelis flammea*	Y	Y	Y
Hoary redpoll	*Carduelis hornemanni*	Y	Y	Y
Pine siskin	*Carduelis pinus*	N	Y	?
American goldfinch	*Carduelis tristis*	N	Y	N
Old World sparrows				
House sparrow	*Passer domesticus*	Y	Y	Y

GLOSSARY

avian cholera. An infectious disease of birds, also called fowl cholera, caused by bacteria.

benthic invertebrate. An animal without a backbone that lives on the bottom of a lake or ocean, such as a clam or a sea star.

benthivore. An animal that feeds on the bottom of a lake or ocean.

binomial nomenclature. The system through which living things are named using a two-part Latin description (e.g., *Homo sapiens* for humans).

braided river. A larger river that is made up of a network of smaller channels, usually separated by low, often sandy or silty islands.

breeding density. The number of breeding pairs (nests) of a bird species within a certain area, often reported as number of pairs per square kilometre.

brood. The family group of chicks from a single nest.

brood parasitism. A behaviour in which one female lays her eggs in the nest of another female, or has her chicks join another nest or group of chicks, leaving all of the work of hatching the eggs and raising the young to the original nest owner.

carnivore. An animal that eats the flesh of other animals.

carrion. The dead and rotting body of an animal.

chick rearing. The process through which adult birds raise their young after the chicks have hatched.

clutch. The set of eggs in a nest.

colour variant. A colour variation in plumage or body parts that differs from the normal pattern in the species.

convergence zone. A zone in the ocean where two flows of water meet and interact, usually giving a different appearance to the surface water.

convergent evolution. The tendency of distinct organisms living in similar ecological niches to evolve similar physical characteristics.

COSEWIC. The Committee on the Status of Endangered Wildlife in Canada, a group that takes information from different sources and makes recommendations to the government on how rare (or in trouble) a species may be.

crèche. A large group of young birds (usually waterfowl) comprising the broods of many different females.

crustacean. An aquatic invertebrate that usually breathes through gills and has a segmented body, an exoskeleton, and often legs.

cryptic. (of colouration or markings) Hidden or obscure; serving to camouflage a bird in its natural habitat.

dimorphic. See also sexual dimorphism. Typically occurring in two different forms, such as in one dark form and one light form.

ecological niche. The status or position of an organism within its environment, community, and food web; its position or role in nature.

distraction display. A behavioural display exhibited by birds to draw the attention of a predator to them, and away from their nest or young.

endangered. A status assigned to very rare animals by COSEWIC and the government under the *Species at Risk Act*, indicating that the species is in trouble.

endothermic. (of a bird or animal) Capable of the internal generation of heat; able to maintain a near-constant internal temperature despite the environmental temperature.

estuary. Shallow, coastal bay area where river currents meet the ocean's tide.

floe edge. The productive region where fast sea ice meets open water.

forage. To feed.

forked. (of a tail) Having a deep V-shape in the middle, with two long, pointed projections on the outside; bifurcated.

gregarious. Tending to form a group with others of the same species; sociable.

grinning patch. The pattern and colour around the bill of a snow goose, which makes the bird look like it is smiling.

herbivore. An animal that feeds mainly on plants.

incubation. The process of sitting on eggs to keep them warm and help them develop into chicks.

insectivore. An animal that feeds mostly on insects.

intertidal zone. The ocean zone between high tide and low tide, which for part of the day is underwater and for the other part is exposed to the air.

kleptoparasitism. A strategy of feeding where an animal steals the food that another animal has captured.

lek. A small area of ground used for a communal breeding display by males of certain bird species.

molluscivore. An animal that feeds mostly on mollusks.

monomorphic. (of an animal species) Having little or no variation in size and appearance.

moult. (of a bird) Shed old feathers to make way for new ones.

morph. Each of several variant forms of an animal or plant.

nape. The back of the neck of a bird.

nunatak. A mountain peak that is surrounded by glacial ice.

omnivore. An animal that regularly eats other plants and animal flesh.

piscivore. An animal that feeds mostly on fish.

planktivore. An animal that feeds primarily on plankton.

polyandry. A breeding system in which a female has more than one male mate at a time, or in which a female mates with more than one male in a breeding season.

polygyny. A breeding system in which a male has more than one female mate at a time, or in which a male mates with more than one female in a breeding season.

polymorphic. (of an animal species) Having different forms; displaying variation in size and appearance.

polynya. An area of predictable, recurrent open water surrounded by sea ice, usually formed by currents or upwelling.

predator. An organism that hunts or kills other organisms for food; can be either a carnivore or an omnivore.

promiscuous. (of certain birds) Characterized by frequent mating with several different partners.

pyriform. (of an egg) Having one large, round end and one narrow, pointy end.

pelagic zone. The open water zone of a lake or ocean that is not close to the shore nor to the bottom of the water.

primary feathers. The long outer flight feathers on a bird's wing.

polygon formation. A type of patterned ground formation created by differential melting of ice in the active surface layer, leading to large, flat, usually wet tundra bordered in a polygon by a raised, muddy area.

race. A local population or group of a species distinguished by similar features, but still capable of fully interbreeding with other races within the species.

raft. A large group of birds (usually waterfowl) gathered together on a large lake or the ocean.

scavenger. An animal that feeds on dead, discarded, leftover, or decaying material.

semi-colonial. (of a bird species) Not nesting in dense breeding colonies, but still occurring in patchy, somewhat increased breeding densities.

sexual dimorphism. A physical dichotomy between males and females of the same species.

special concern. A status assigned to some uncommon animals by COSEWIC and the government under the *Species at Risk Act.*

Species at Risk Act. A Canadian law that identifies and protects rare wildlife in Canada.

taxonomy. The branch of science concerned with classifying organisms into groups based on similar characteristics, genetics, or evolutionary history.

threatened. A status assigned to rare animals by COSEWIC and the government under the *Species at Risk Act*, usually indicating that the animals are in trouble.

trans-equatorial migration. The movement of birds from their breeding grounds in the northern hemisphere to their wintering grounds in the southern hemisphere (i.e., across the equator).

undulating. (of birds) Moving up and down like waves when flying.

upwelling. An oceanographic phenomenon usually involving the movement of dense, cool, nutrient-rich water from the ocean's depths to the surface.

zooplankton. Tiny, free-floating predatory organisms in water that include crustaceans and tiny fish larvae.

BIBLIOGRAPHY

Bart, J. R., and V. H. Johnston. *Arctic Shorebirds in North America: A Decade of Monitoring.* Berkeley: University of California Press, 2012.

Bird, D. *Birds of Canada.* Toronto: Dorling Kindersley Ltd., 2010.

Cornell Lab of Ornithology. "The Birds of North America Online." Cornell Lab of Ornithology and American Ornithologists' Union, 2011. http://bna.birds.cornell.edu/bna/.

Egevang, C., I. J. Stenhouse, R. A. Phillips, A. Petersen, J. W. Fox, and J. R. D. Silk. "Tracking of Arctic terns *Sterna paradisaea* reveals longest animal migration." *Proceedings of the National Academy of Science* 107 (2010): 2078–2081.

Gilchrist, H. G., M. L. Mallory, and F. R. Merkel. "Can traditional ecological knowledge contribute to wildlife management? Case studies of migratory birds." *Ecology and Society* 10, no. 1 (2005): 20. http://www.ecologyandsociety.org/vol10/iss1/art20/.

Latour, P. B., J. Leger, J. E. Hines, M. L. Mallory, D. L. Mulders, H. G. Gilchrist, P. A. Smith, and D. L. Dickson. *Key migratory bird terrestrial habitat sites in the Northwest Territories and Nunavut,* 2008. Canadian Wildlife Service occasional paper no. 114.

Lepage, D., D. N. Nettleship, and A. Reed. Birds of Bylot Island and adjacent Baffin Island, Northwest Territories, Canada, 1979-1997. *Arctic* 51 (1998): 125–141.

Mallory, M. L., and A. J. Fontaine. *Key marine habitat sites for migratory birds in Nunavut and the Northwest Territories,* 2004. Canadian Wildlife Service occasional paper no. 109.

Mallory, M. L., J. Akearok and A. J. Fontaine. *Community knowledge on the distribution and abundance of species at risk in southern Baffin Island, Nunavut, Canada,* 2001. Canadian Wildlife Service technical report no. 363.

Mallory, M. L., J. E. Hines, and H. G. Gilchrist. *Status of migratory game birds in the Nunavut Settlement Area,* 2004. Environment Canada Report to Nunavut Wildlife Management Board.

Mallory, M. L., A. J. Gaston, H. G. Gilchrist, G. J. Robertson, and B. L. Braune. "Effects of climate change, altered sea-ice distribution and seasonal phenology on marine birds." In *A Little Less Arctic: Changes to Top Predators in the World's Largest Northern Inland Sea, Hudson Bay*, edited by S. Ferguson, L. Loseto, and M. Mallory, 179–195. The Netherlands: Springer-Verlag, 2010.

Priest, H., and P. J. Usher. *The Nunavut Wildlife Harvest Study.* Iqaluit, NU: Nunavut Wildlife Management Board, August 2004.

Richards, J., and T. White. *Birds of Nunavut: A Checklist.* Yellowknife, NT: Canadian Wildlife Service, November 2008.

Scott, S. L., ed. *Field Guide to the Birds of North America.* Washington, DC: National Geographic Society, 1987.

Van Meurs, R., and J. F. Splettstoesser. "Farthest North polar bear (*Ursus maritimus*)" (letter to the editor). *Arctic* 56, no. 3 (2003): 309.

Wendt, J. S., and M. Wyndham. *Birds of Nunavut.* Iqaluit, NU: Baffin Divisional Board of Education, 1997.